THE HISPANIC SERIES

UNDER THE EDITORSHIP OF

JOHN D. FITZ-GERALD, PH.D., LITT.D.

PROFESSOR OF ROMANCE PHILOLOGY, UNIVERSITY
OF ILLINOIS; MEMBER OF THE HISPANIC SOCIETY
OF AMERICA; CORRESPONDIENTE DE LAS REALES
ACADEMIAS ESPAÑOLA, DE LA HISTORIA DE MADRID,
DE BUENAS LETRAS DE BARCELONA, SEVILLANA
DE BUENAS LETRAS, GALLEGA, E HISPANO-AMERI-
CANA DE CÁDIZ; ACADÉMICO HONORARIO DE LA
ACADEMIA NACIONAL DE CUBA; COMENDADOR CON
PLACA DE LA REAL ORDEN DE ISABEL LA CATÓLICA

A PRIMER OF
SPANISH PRONUNCIATION

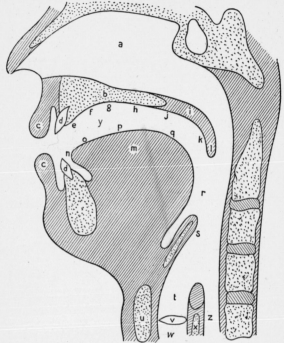

FIG. 1. The Organs of Speech

a. Nasal cavity
b. Hard palate
c. Lips
d. Teeth
e. Alveoles
f. Hard palate, forward
g. Hard palate, middle
h. Hard palate, back
i. Soft palate (Velum)
j. Soft palate, forward
k. Soft palate, back
l. Uvula
m. Tongue

n. Tip of tongue
o. Front (Blade) of tongue
p. Middle (Ridge) of tongue
q. Back of tongue
r. Pharynx
s. Epiglottis
t. Larynx
u. Adam's apple
v. Glottis; Vocal cords
w. Trachea (Windpipe)
x. Cricoid cartilage
y. Oral cavity
z. Esophagus

A PRIMER

OF

SPANISH PRONUNCIATION

BY

TOMÁS NAVARRO TOMÁS

PROFESSOR OF EXPERIMENTAL PHONETICS IN THE
CENTRO DE ESTUDIOS HISTÓRICOS, MADRID

AND

AURELIO M. ESPINOSA

PROFESSOR OF ROMANIC LANGUAGES
STANFORD UNIVERSITY

WITH A PRÓLOGO BY

RAMÓN MENÉNDEZ PIDAL

DIRECTOR OF THE CENTRO DE ESTUDIOS HISTÓRICOS

BENJ. H. SANBORN & CO.

CHICAGO   NEW YORK   BOSTON

1926

PREFACE

A PRIMER OF SPANISH PRONUNCIATION is a brief introduction to the pronunciation of the Spanish language as spoken today by the educated people of Old and New Castile. While the fundamental basis of this pronunciation is Castilian the authors call it Spanish because in general it is so called by modern Spanish grammarians and phoneticians and because Castilian speech, Castilian pronunciation, Castilian idiom, etc., are terms now used for the corresponding phenomena that occur in the country districts of Castile among the uneducated people. The correct standard Spanish pronunciation as described in our *Primer* is in its essential features the pronunciation that is heard among the educated people of Old and New Castile, at the court of Alfonso XIII, at the Universidad Central and other centres of Spanish learning and culture, at the theatres, churches, tribunals, etc., of the two Castiles. In a wider sense it is also the pronunciation of educated Spaniards of all Spain and many parts of Spanish America.

v

Since this *Primer* is only a brief introduction for the use of beginners many of the minute details of Spanish pronunciation have been entirely omitted. For pedagogical reasons the number of phonetic symbols used for the various sounds has been limited as far as possible. In some cases there may be in this respect a difference of opinion among teachers, but the authors have decided to be conservative and have chosen to have fewer rather than more symbols than the average teacher of Spanish pronunciation would advocate for the use of beginners. For these reasons we have not used separate symbols, for example, for the open sounds of i and u, but teachers who understand Spanish pronunciation well and who believe these open sounds can be taught to our high school and college pupils may not only teach the open sounds of these vowels but also use separate symbols for them, the i and u with the conventional marks used for all open vowels.

The phonetic symbols used in our *Primer* are those used in the *Revista de Filología Española*. These symbols differ from those used by the Association Phonétique Internationale in the case of ẹ, ọ, ĉ, ḷ, ṇ, r̄, ŷ, and these have been preferred by the authors because they are the ones commonly used in the standard journals and treatises on Romance philology and linguistics, for example, in *Revista de Filología Española*, above mentioned,

Revue Hispanique, Rivista di Filología, the *Grammaire des Langues Romanes* of Meyer-Lübke, and in Gröber's *Grundriss der Romanischen Philologie*.

The ambitious student and the teacher who wish to continue their study of Spanish pronunciation should consult the book of the senior author, *Manual de Pronunciación Española*, Madrid, 1918 (second edition, 1921),[1] a more detailed study that has been in the main the basis for the preparation of our *Primer*.

Tomás Navarro Tomás
Aurelio M. Espinosa

[1] See *Romanic Review*, Volume XIII, 1922, pages 88–91.

CONTENTS

PRÓLOGO

A Primer of Spanish Pronunciation. ¿Y por qué *Spanish*, preguntará alguno, para quien *Castilian* habría sonado a cosa más noble, más puristamente castiza? Pues porque la formación de la más importante lengua literaria de España, aunque es debida principalmente a Castilla, es también fruto de la colaboración esencial de las otras regiones. La misma Real Academia que, aunque usando siempre ambos nombres de lengua *española* y *castellana* prefería éste último, ha adoptado por fin, después de madura discusión, el nombre de lengua *española*, como más propio.

La pronunciación española no es la vulgar del pueblo de Castilla ni la del vulgo de ninguna otra región. Los castellanos no pronuncian todos de igual modo; los andaluces tampoco; los hispanoamericanos se diferencian bastante entre sí. ¿Quién podría imponer la norma? Ninguno de un modo absolutamente general. La lengua española, común a todos, es el resultado de la multisecular colaboración de los hombres cultos de todas las regiones hispánicas, que al expresarse obran constreñidos por la necesidad habitual de usar una lengua superior a la del vulgo y a la de la región, una lengua que les sirva para salir fuera de la intimidad descuidada y del localismo cerrado, y para alcanzar el trato humano más correcto y cortés, más elegante y elevado, más artístico e intelectual.

Las normas de la pronunciación culta las dan a cada instante la conversación culta, la oratoria, la recitación del verso y, sobre todo, la declamación del teatro, arte de gran difusión y popularidad. Y más aun que estos modelos que obran directamente sobre el oído, influye por medio de la vista la ortografía : su acción no se halla cortamente limitada, como la de la palabra hablada, al momento y al lugar reducido donde se produce, sino que se perpetúa sobre el papel y se propaga con la imprenta a ambos hemisferios del mundo.

Por fortuna, la ortografía española es, sin duda, la más perfecta entre las ortografías de las grandes lenguas literarias, por su exactitud, por su precisión, por su sencillez. Aunque no llega, como no llega ninguna ortografía tradicional, a expresar al pormenor todos los matices de la correcta pronunciación, representa con fidelidad admirable la pronunciación selecta que tradicionalmente se ha aceptado para la gran literatura común a todos los hispano-dicentes, pronunciación que se comprueba sobre todo en el ajuste de las rimas poéticas.

La ortografía común representa la pronunciación más literaria, la que distingue la *ll* de la *y*, y la *s* de la *z*, según las rimas de los versos piden.

Pero la pronunciación culta nunca es enteramente uniforme, ni aun dentro de un reducido país. Hay siempre discrepancias admisibles, que no suenan a ignorancia o tosquedad. Así por ejemplo, fijándonos en discrepancias de gran bulto, los castellanos relajan demasiado la pronunciación de la *d* en la terminación — *ado*, y dicen *cansa(ð)o;* los andaluces y americanos sesean, confundiendo la *s* y la *z*. Ninguno de estos dos defectos es tenido por zafio o grosero; están admitidos en la pronunciación docta. No obstante, el castellano al hablar en público corregirá su habitual abandono y dirá *cansaðo;* y el andaluz o el americano, si bien para la oratoria conserva su seseo, habrá de desecharlo sin embargo cuando se exija más esmero aún; al recitar versos o al interpretar un papel de alta comedia o de drama, se esforzará en distinguir *s* y *z*.

Admitidas ciertas divergencias como éstas, que existen, y mucho mayores, en todos los idiomas aun en los de menor extensión geográfica, no puede decirse que haya oposición entre lo castellano y lo hispanoamericano. Este antagonismo que algunos establecen y exageran, sea por sincera desorientación, sea por servir a intereses o pasiones particulares contra el puro interés humano, cien-

tífico y literario, queda resuelto dentro de la unidad superior de la lengua española culta y literaria.
La pronunciación culta es común en lo fundamental,
y hasta en la inmensa mayoría de los detalles, a
españoles e hispanoamericanos instruidos, por cima
de las diferencias regionales que existen entre castellanos, leoneses, andaluces, argentinos, mejica-
nos etc. Estas diferencias, lo repetimos, son menores
que las de otros idiomas, y sin duda que esta unidad
fundamental del español, mayor por ejemplo que la
de las otras dos grandes lenguas Europeas extendidas
por América, se debe en gran parte a la sencillez,
claridad y firmeza de nuestro sistema vocálico.

La enseñanza del idioma es la encargada de acer-
car en todo lo posible las inevitables divergencias.
Hay, por ejemplo, muchas regiones que confunden
la *ll* y la *y*. Esta confusión, llamada yeísmo, está
asímismo admitida, aunque menos que el seseo;
tiende a mirarse como poco culta, y por lo tanto, a
corregirse. Una inteligente presión de la enseñanza
escolar en favor de la distinción de ambos sonidos,
ayudada de una exacta descripción fonética de la
ll, podrá ser eficazmente restauradora de esta arti-
culación en los paises que la tienen más o menos
olvidada, y tal restauración, en efecto, se generaliza
ya en algunas regiones de España y de América.

Por eso un buen manual de fonética práctica,
como el de Navarro Tomás, es de grande valor;

hasta reviste un verdadero interés social, pues contribuye a la mejor conservación del lenguaje, instrumento de comercio humano que a todos interesa mantener en perfecto estado, sin mellas ni moho que hagan su funcionamiento más torpe, su uso más duro.

El *Manual* de Navarro Tomás es un eficaz medio de propagar un tipo depurado de pronunciación, el que mejor representa el habla culta y selecta, exenta a la vez de vulgarismo o particularismo familiar y de toda afectación altisonante. Su análisis y descripción de los sonidos se funda siempre en muy detenidos trabajos experimentales de laboratorio, o en muy comprobadas observaciones acústicas; nunca se hallarán en él esas alocadas generalizaciones mal basadas en fantásticas percepciones empíricas y propias solo para sorprender un momento de descuido del lector inteligente. Basta recordar el riguroso método científico de las abundantes monografías que ha publicado Navarro Tomás. Por todas partes en el *Manual* de Navarro Tomás se encuentra esa sólida erudición, esa claridad de inteligencia, ese ponderado acierto y buen gusto que tanto caracterizan la doctrina del autor, y tanta eficacia dan a su enseñanza desde hace muchos años.

Pero ese *Manual* sirve solo para profesores y estudiantes adelantados. Era preciso darle una forma menos difícil. Y he aquí la presente abreviación que se publica en inglés y se dirige a los extranjeros principiantes. En esta adaptación colabora con el Sr. Navarro Tomás el Profesor A. M. Espinosa, cuyos doctos trabajos sobre prosodia de la lengua española culta y sobre fonética dialectal, así como su experiencia en la cátedra, le autorizan señaladamente para esta labor delicada de iniciar en la buena doctrina a los estudiantes de habla inglesa, teniendo muy especial cuenta con los defectos que son entre ellos más corrientes.

Los Señores Navarro Tomás y Espinosa, en este *Primer of Spanish Pronunciation*, han simplificado con todo acierto las cuestiones. No hablan, por ejemplo, de varias clases de *a* palatal o velar, ni de *i* ni de *u* abiertas o cerradas, pero conservan la más importante distinción entre *e* y *ę*, *o* y *ǫ*. Por otra parte, las discrepancias entre la *s* dental y la alveolar, el seseo y el yeísmo, van tratados con la necesaria tolerancia y se admiten como variedades aceptables en la lengua culta. No se impone fanáticamente la modalidad *castellana*, sino que se atiende al *español* de las personas ilustradas. Claro es que se indica como preferente la pronunciación castellana, por ser la más conforme con la tradición literaria y con la ortografía general. En verdad, el aprendiz extranjero, puesto a escoger entre el seseo y la distinción de *s* y *z*, obrará desacertadamente si elige la modalidad menos literaria, la que no está comprobada por las rimas de toda la poesía española. Bueno que el andaluz y el americano no se desvivan por corregir su seseo, ya que es aceptable también en Castilla como modalidad culta; pero será insensato que quien va de nuevo a aprender el español, sin tener sobre sí el peso de una tradición, no aprenda la distinción de *s* y *z*, que además de ser mucho más aceptable a su vez en Andalucía o en América, es preferible para el buen uso de la ortografía y para el estudio de la poesía española.

A Primer of Spanish Pronunciation, tratando todas estas cuestiones con gran madurez y buen sentido, con notable claridad y exactitud, fundado siempre en muy especiales observaciones hechas con todo rigor científico, habrá de prestar seguramente los mayores beneficios a la enseñanza.

R. MENÉNDEZ PIDAL

MADRID,
    Junio de 1925.

A PRIMER OF SPANISH PRONUNCIATION

CHAPTER I

ELEMENTARY PRINCIPLES

DESCRIPTION OF SPEECH-SOUNDS

1. The organs of speech. The organs of speech are the lungs, the windpipe or trachea, the larynx with the vocal chords, the pharynx, the nasal cavities, and the mouth with the tongue, the lips, the teeth, the palate, etc. See Figure 1, frontispiece.

2. Speech-sounds. In the production of the sounds of any language the chief factor is breathing. The breath is expelled from the lungs, undergoes various modifications in the larynx and in the organs of speech above the larynx, and produces the different speech-sounds.

3. Voiced and voiceless sounds. When the breath is expelled from the lungs it passes out through the windpipe or trachea into the larynx. Across the larynx are stretched two muscular ligaments, called the vocal chords. When the breath passes through

1

the larynx the vocal chords may remain open and neutral. The resulting sound is then voiceless breath or what is ordinarily called mere breath. If, however, as the breath passes through the larynx the vocal chords are partially closed and stretched, producing a series of musical vibrations which we call voice, the resulting sound is voiced breath or voice.

4. Vowels. When in the production of a sound as described in § 3 the vocal chords vibrate and the breath is further modified by the position of the tongue, lips, etc., but without producing audible friction, the resulting sound is called a vowel. A vowel, therefore, may be defined as voiced breath modified by the organs of speech above the larynx but without audible friction.[1]

5. Consonants. When in the production of a sound as described in § 3, whether voiced or voiceless, the breath is further modified by the organs of speech above the larynx to the extent that the friction is plainly audible, the resulting sound is called a consonant. A consonant, therefore, may be defined as voiced or voiceless breath modified by the organs of speech above the larynx and with audible friction.[1]

---

[1] All vowels are voiced, therefore, while consonants may be either voiced or voiceless. By placing the thumb and the index finger on the larynx or Adam's apple one can easily feel the vibrations of the vocal chords when a vowel or a voiced consonant is pronounced. By pronouncing rapidly ssss, zzzz, ssss, zzzz one can clearly feel the

6. Semivowels or semiconsonants. When in the production of some sounds the audible friction and the voice are in about equal proportions the resulting sound is called a semivowel or a semiconsonant. The *i* and *u* in the Spanish words **aire**, **causa** are semivowels; in the words **bien**, **bueno** they are semiconsonants.

7. The place of articulation. Vowels and consonants are often classified according to the place of articulation. In the mouth cavity the various positions of the tongue, teeth, lips, etc., determine the articulation of speech-sounds. Speech-sounds may be classified, therefore, according to the place where these modifications are made. The general names by which we classify most speech-sounds are based on the place of articulation : bilabial, labial (the lips), labio-dental (lips and teeth), interdental (between the teeth), dental (teeth), alveolar (alveoles), palatal (palate), velar (velum or veil of the palate), uvular (uvula), etc. In most of these terminologies we have indicated only the passive organ involved in the production of the sound in question. The tongue, which is the active organ in the production of most sounds, determines the exact place of articulation in most cases.

vibrations in the voiced **zzzz**, and by pronouncing rapidly **sszz, sszz, sszz, sszz** one can learn to feel the distinction clearly between the voiceless **ss** and the voiced **zz**.

8. The manner of articulation. Explosives and continuants. Speech-sounds may be classified also according to the manner of articulation. In the pronunciation of the consonants the stoppage of the breath through the adjustment of the tongue or lips may be complete or partial. If the stoppage is complete and then suddenly broken, the consonant is called an explosive, for example, English *p*, *b*, *t*, *d*, *k*, *g*. If, however, the stoppage is partial, allowing the breath to pass through a narrow passage, the consonant is called a continuant, for example, English *s*, *z*, *f*, *v*. According to the manner of articulation we may classify consonants, therefore, not only as voiced and voiceless, but also as explosives and continuants.

Semiexplosives. In the articulation of some consonants there is a complete stoppage of the breath, as in the case of the explosives, but the explosion is momentaneous and the tongue contact is then slowly and gradually removed, producing a slight friction. These consonants are called semiexplosives. English *ch*, *j*, are examples of semiexplosives.

Spanish Syllabication

9. In studying Spanish pronunciation it is first of all important to have an accurate knowledge of the rules governing Spanish syllabication. It is also important to distinguish carefully between orthographic syllabication, the formal rules of the grammarians, and phonetic syllabication, which is the way Spanish people actually divide words into syllables in speaking. Orthographic syllabication is generally, though not always, based on phonetic syllabication. The principal rules of the orthographic syllabication are the following :

a. A single consonant between two vowels begins a syllable :

ca-sa	a-re-na	a-ba-ni-co
co-me	co-mi-da	ci-vi-li-za-do

b. The digraphs *ch*, *ll*, *rr*, which represent single consonantal sounds, also begin a syllable :

ha-cha	e-lla	ca-rro
le-che	ca-lle	pe-rro

c. The groups consonant + *l* or *r* (except *rl*, *sl*, *tl*, *sr*) also begin a syllable :

ha-bla	a-fli-gi-do	a-pli-car	a-gra-da	pa-dre
a-brir	o-fre-cer	a-pri-sa	de-cla-ra	a-trás

d. When the groups *rl*, *sl*, *tl*, *sr*, or any other two consonants not coming under the rules of paragraphs **b** and **c**, come between vowels one consonant goes with the preceding syllable and the other goes with the following syllable :

ac-to	con-cep-to	cas-ti-llo	tres-cien-tos
fir-me	per-der-se	at-le-ta	en-ten-der
bas-ta	con-tar-nos	Is-ra-el	des-truc-ción

e. When more than two consonants occur between vowels only the last consonant or the two consonants of the inseparable groups of § **9 c** begin a syllable :

mez-cla	es-truc-tu-ra	trans-plan-tar
ex-pre-sar	sor-pren-der	ins-pi-ra-ción

f. Prefixes must be kept intact even when the usual rules are violated :

ab-ro-gar	en-al-te-cer
des-a-tar	sub-le-var

g. When two strong vowels[1] come together they form different syllables, the second one beginning a new syllable :

le-a	lo-a	Ra-fa-el	le-al-tad
ve-a-mos	le-ón	pa-se-o	ca-e-mos

h. When a strong vowel is immediately followed by a weak vowel they form one syllable, a diphthong :

au-tor	ai-re	pei-ne	deu-da	hoy
cau-ti-vo	cai-go	oi-go	hay	ley

[1] The vowels *a*, *e*, *o* are called strong vowels, and the vowels *i*, *u* (and *y* when a vowel as in *ley*) are called weak vowels.

i. When the vowels of the groups of § **9 h** retain their syllabic value and form separate syllables the weak vowel bears the stress and has the accent mark:

ca-í-do	ma-íz	pa-ís
ba-úl	re-ír	le-í

j. When a weak vowel is followed by any vowel, whether strong or weak, it loses its syllabic value and becomes semiconsonantal. The *i* becomes **j** and the *u* becomes **w**. See § **6** and §§ **26, 35.**

tie-ne	es-tu-dia	cui-da-do
siem-pre	bue-no	ciu-dad
va-ria-do	puer-ta	cui-ta
lec-ción	cuan-do	fui-mos

k. When the vowels of the groups of § **9 j** retain their syllabic values and form different syllables the first bears the stress and has the accent mark:

dí-a	con-ti-nú-a	ha-cí-a
fí-an	flú-ido	has-tí-o

10. Phonetic syllabication. Although phonetic syllabication is the basis of the orthographic syllabication and is in the main the same, the following differences should be carefully observed.

a. Rule § **9 f** for orthographic syllabication, which is based on etymology and not on phonetic law, does not apply :

a-bro-gar	e-nal-te-cer
de-sa-tar	su-ble-var

b. Within a phonic or breath[1] group the final consonant of a word goes with the initial vowel or diphthong of the following word and forms a syllable with it, as if it were intervocalic within a word :

mis ojos	=	mi-so-jos
un año	=	u-na-ño
con ella	=	co-ne-lla
los osos	=	lo-so-sos
con el hombre	=	co-ne-lom-**bre**
el hado, helado	=	e-la-do
en ojo, enojo	=	e-no-jo
las aves, la sabes	=	la-sa-bes
el hecho, helecho	=	e-le-cho
en aguas, enaguas	=	e-na-guas

ACCENT OR STRESS

11. We shall treat here of accent or stress in its simplest form, namely, accent in isolated words. In Spanish the matter of accent is extremely important.

[1] A phonic or breath group is a word or group of words pronounced between pauses.

In English the accented syllable of a word usually bears most of the stress and the other syllable or syllables are pronounced with very weak stress or are often slurred. In Spanish, although stress accent is strong and the accented syllable bears most of the stress all the vowels of a word are pronounced clearly and with the same care as the accented vowels. English-speaking students should bear this in mind constantly in studying Spanish pronunciation. It is very important to pronounce from the beginning all the vowels of a word correctly, giving each one its clear quality and not slurring any of them, as is often done in English.

12. But in spite of the fact that in Spanish all the vowels of a word are pronounced fully and clearly, stress accent is very important and the Spanish ear is very sensitive to it. Every word has a fixed accent on one of its vowels and placing the accent where it does not belong is an unpardonable error. From the very beginning of the study of Spanish, therefore, great care should be exercised in pronouncing Spanish words with the proper and correct accentuation.

13. The principal accent rules are the following:

a. Words that end in a vowel or in the consonants **n** or **s** are stressed on the syllable before the last, i.e. the penult:

| casa | comida | amenaza | comidas | tienes |
| loma | comprado | equipaje | equipajes | tienen |

b. Words that end in a consonant (including *y*), except *n* or *s*, are stressed on the last syllable:

| papel | comer | feliz | humanidad | reloj |
| contar | usted | feroz | comprender | Echegaray |

c. Words that do not conform to the above rules have a written accent mark (') over the vowel that bears the stress:

| acción | inglés | lápiz | último | compró |
| lección | francés | fértil | ánimo | canté |

d. Nouns and adjectives that end in an accented vowel + *n* or *s* and that have, therefore, the accent on the final syllable, drop the accent mark in the plural or when the feminine –a is added, although the stress remains on the same syllable. This is done in order to conform with § **13 a**:

	acción	acciones	
	lección	lecciones	
inglés	ingleses	inglesa	inglesas
alemán	alemanes	alemana	alemanas

OPEN AND CLOSED SYLLABLES

14. An open syllable is one that ends in a vowel or diphthong. In the following words all the syllables are open:

ha-bla	tie-ne	ha-bi-ta-do	ci-vi-li-za-do	pei-ne
co-me	due-le	pro-me-ti-do	pe-tri-fi-ca-do	cai-go

15. A closed syllable is one that ends in a consonant or consonants. In the following words all the syllables are closed:

con-tar	sen-tir	com-pren-der	in-sis-tir	sol
per-der	fir-mar	con-tem-plar	sus-ten-tar	con

16. It should be observed that in many nouns the singular has a final open syllable that becomes closed in the plural, while in many others the singular has a final closed syllable that becomes medial and open in the plural:

a.	ni-ño	ni-ños	hom-bre	hom-bres
	ma-no	ma-nos	li-bro	li-bros
b.	sol	so-les	se-ñor	se-ño-res
	don	do-nes	ac-ción	ac-cio-nes

NOTE. — The question of open and closed syllables is of the greatest importance in the study of Spanish pronunciation, particularly in the application of the rules for the open and closed vowels. A closed syllable that is final in a word becomes open when it comes immediately before the initial vowel of a following word in the same phonic group. In order to determine which syllables are open and which are closed it is of course necessary to know the rules that govern Spanish syllabication, §§ **9, 10.**

THE SPANISH ALPHABET

17. The signs or characters of the Spanish alphabet together with their usual names are given below.

a	a	*n*	ene
b	be	*ñ*	eñe
c	ce	*o*	o
ch	che	*p*	pe
d	de	*q*	cu
e	e	*r*	ere
f	efe	*rr*	erre
g	ge	*s*	ese
h	hache	*t*	te
i	i	*u*	u
j	jota	*v*	ve, uve
k	ka	*w*	doble u, uve doble
l	ele	*x*	equis
ll	elle	*y*	ye, i griega
m	eme	*z*	zeta, zeda

NOTE. — The Royal Spanish Academy no longer recognizes *rr* as a separate letter of the alphabet. See its *Gramática de la Lengua Castellana*, Madrid, 1920, page 9.

TABLE OF PHONETIC SYMBOLS

18. The following table gives a complete list of the phonetic symbols used in this book.

Vowels

a	a in padre	ǫ	o in flor
e	e in eso	u	u in luna
ę	e in ser		
i	i in pido	i̯	i in aire ⎤ semi-
o	o in hora	u̯	u in causa ⎦ vowels

' when placed over a vowel indicates accent or stress.

Consonants

b	b in hombre	ŋ	n in tengo
ƀ	b in lobo	ṇ	ñ in año
ĉ	ch in leche	p	p in padre
θ	z in mozo	r	r in hora
d	d in cuando	r̄	rr in carro
đ	d in todo	s	s in casa
f	f in fácil	z	s in rasgo
g	g in tengo	z	z in juzgar
ǥ	g in hago	t	t in bota
k	c in casa	x	j in caja
l	l in luna	y	y in mayo
ḷ	ll in calle	ŷ	y in conyuge
m	m in toma		
ṃ	n in enfermo	j	i in bien ⎤ semi-
n	n in mano	w	u in bueno ⎦ consonants

CHAPTER II

VOWELS

General Remarks

19. The articulation of Spanish vowels. The position of the tongue in the mouth cavity determines the quality of each vowel sound. The vowels that are articulated in the front half of the mouth cavity are called front or palatal vowels, while the vowels that are articulated in the back half of the mouth cavity are called back or velar vowels.

In the articulation of the front vowels the tongue gradually moves forward and is raised towards the front palate. The Spanish vowels ę, e, i are front vowels. In the articulation of the back vowels the tongue is gradually drawn back and is raised towards the velum or soft palate. The Spanish vowels ǫ, o, u are back vowels. In the articulation of the vowel **a** the tongue remains in a neutral position.

20. Open and closed vowels. Within each one of these two divisions vowels are divided into open and closed vowels, according to the degree to which

14

the tongue is tensed and raised towards the palate.
The distance between the tongue and the palate is
greater in the open vowels than in the closed vowels.
The air escapes, therefore, through a wider or more
open channel in the open vowels and through a
narrower or more closed channel in the closed
vowels. In Spanish the most open vowel is **a**
and the most closed vowels are **i** for the front vowels
and **u** for the back vowels.

21. The vowel triangle. The articulation of the
Spanish vowels according to their tongue positions
may be represented by an
inverted triangle. See Figure 2. The upper vertices
of the triangle occupy the
points of articulation of the
front or palatal vowel **i** and
the back or velar vowel **u**,
and the lower vertex occu-
pies the point of articulation
of the vowel **a**. Between
the vowel **a** and the vowel **i** are the vowels **ę** and
e, and between the vowel **a** and the vowel **u** are the
vowels **ǫ** and **o**.

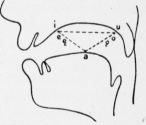

Fig. 2. Articulation of the
Spanish vowels according to
the tongue position.

22. In pronouncing the Spanish vowels the student
should very carefully avoid giving them the corresponding or approximate English values which are
given only as a basis of comparison. No Spanish

vowel is exactly like a corresponding English vowel. Spanish vowels are pronounced clearly and distinctly. They are uniform in quality throughout their articulation and the closed vowels never have the English diphthongal character. The English off-glide of such vowels as English *o* and *e* in *go* and *they* should be avoided in the Spanish closed vowels **o** and **e** from the beginning and persistently. The English closed *o* and *e* are pronounced more like the Spanish diphthongs **ou, ei.**

The position of the lips is also important. In the articulation of the front vowels the lips form an oblong opening which becomes longer and narrower as the vowel is more closed. In the articulation of the back vowels the lips are rounded and the opening is gradually reduced as the vowel is more closed.

23. Quality and quantity of final unaccented vowels. English-speaking students in learning a foreign language are very careless in the pronunciation of final unaccented vowels. In Spanish great care should be exercised in the pronunciation of these vowels. Final unaccented vowels are usually pronounced almost as clearly and distinctly as in any other position. Accented vowels are not necessarily long in Spanish. In fact a final unaccented vowel may be often not only as long as, but even longer than, an accented vowel.

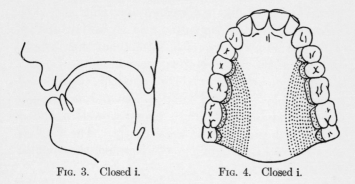

FIG. 3.   Closed i.   FIG. 4.   Closed i.

FRONT VOWELS

24. Closed i.   Orthography i, phonetic symbol i.
The tip of the tongue rests on the lower teeth while
the front is raised towards the hard palate. The
sides of the tongue touch the palate widely, leaving
in the center a narrow opening. The corners of
the lips are drawn back. See Figures 3 and 4.
Spanish closed i is similar to English *ee* in *see*, but
its quality is uniform throughout and it does not
end in a diphthongal glide.

Spanish *i* is closed in all open syllables, and with
the variation discussed below also in closed syllables.

EXAMPLES

piso	píso	escribí	eskribí
niño	níṇo	castillo	kastíḷo
pica	píka	visitar	bisitár

25. Open i. In most closed syllables, especially before *l*, *r*, and *s*, Spanish *i* has a more open quality than the closed i described above. The tongue is lowered a little from the position assumed for i and the distance between the tongue and the palate is consequently greater. This open quality of Spanish *i* is a sound halfway between the closed i and the open quality of English *i* in *hiss*. It is very difficult for English-speaking students to pronounce Spanish open *i* even approximately correctly. Experience shows that they almost invariably relapse into the more open *i* of English *hiss*. For these reasons this sound is represented also by the symbol i as in the case of *i* in open syllables. The teacher of Spanish, however, who is thoroughly familiar with this open sound of Spanish *i* in closed syllables may very properly teach it.

EXAMPLES

firme	fírme	insistir	insistír
diste	díste	principal	prinθipál
decir	deθír	importante	impǫrtánte

For the open and short *i* of the diphthongs *ai*, *oi*, etc., see § **36**.

26. Semiconsonantal i. Orthography i, phonetic symbol j. The front of the tongue is raised very closely towards the hard palate and the sides touch the palate over a wide area, leaving a very narrow passage for the breath. There is a slight friction. The front of the tongue is raised to a position half-way between the tongue position for i and that for y. See Figures 3, 4 and 33, 34. This sound is similar to the English *y* in *you.*

Spanish *i* is semiconsonantal when before a vowel with which it forms a syllable and when preceded by a consonant, that is, in the syllabic group consonant + *i* + vowel.

EXAMPLES

bien	bjén	ciencia	θjénθja
pieza	pjéθa	violencia	bjolénθja
tiene	tjéne	comercio	komę́rθjo

When *i* + vowel is absolutely initial in a syllable the *i* is a pure consonant, as in hielo, pronounced yelo. See § 63.

27. Closed e. Orthography e, phonetic symbol e. The tip of the tongue rests on the lower teeth and the middle of the tongue is raised towards the palate, touching on both sides an area a little smaller than for i. The distance between the tongue and the palate is greater than for i, the mouth is wider open and the lips are slightly drawn back. The muscular tension is quite strong. See Figures 5 and 6. Closed e is similar to English *e* in *they* but without the diphthongal glide.

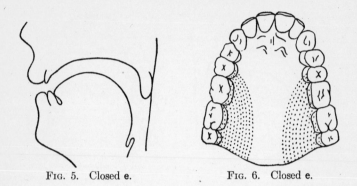

FIG. 5. Closed **e**.　　　FIG. 6. Closed **e**.

Closed **e** is found in open syllables, and in closed syllables before *m*, *n*, *s* (voiceless and voiced), or *x* (= *s*, § **71**). Exceptions are noted below, § **28**.

EXAMPLES

eso	éso	cesta	θésta
pone	póne	tienes	tjénes
leemos	leémọs	pensar	pensár
compré	kọmpré	desde	dézđe
siempre	sjémpre	extraño	estráŋo

28. Open e. Orthography e, phonetic symbol ę. The distance between the tongue and the palate is greater than for **e** and the mouth opened wider. The point of articulation is in the back half of the hard palate. Spanish open **e** is similar to English *e* in *let*. See Figures 7 and 8.

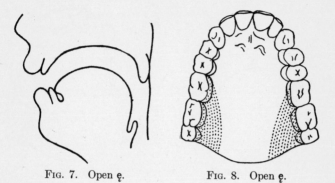

Fig. 7. Open ę.   Fig. 8. Open ę.

Spanish *e* is pronounced ę in the following cases:

1. In closed syllables, except those closed by *m*, *n*, *s*, or *x* (= *s*).
2. When in contact with a trilled *r* (r̄) anywhere.
3. When before the *j* sound (x).
4. In the diphthongs *ei, ey*.

Examples

perder	pęrđę́r	regla	r̄ę́gla
lección	lęgθjǫ́n	tierra	tję́r̄a
directo	dirę́kto	corren	kǫ́r̄ęn
papel	papę́l	deja	dę́xa
concepto	kǫnθę́pto	mejor	męxǫ́r
del	dęl	peine	pę́ine
ser	sę́r	ley	lę́i

The Vowel a

29. Medial a. Orthography a, phonetic symbol a. The tongue lies almost flat in the mouth, with

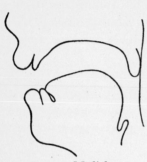

the tip touching the lower teeth and even the gums, and the back is raised slightly towards the soft palate. The mouth is opened wider than in any other Spanish vowel and the distance between the tongue and the palate consequently the greatest. The distance between the teeth

Fig. 9. Medial **a**.

is about ten millimeters. See Figure 9. This sound is between the *a* of English *ask* and the *a* of *father*. Before palatal consonants it approaches more the *a* of *ask*.

Medial **a** is the general sound of Spanish *a* in most cases.

Examples

cama	kárma	callar	kaḷár
cantaba	kantáƀa	cañas	káɲas
pedazo	peđáθo	mayo	máyo
cortar	kọrtár	alzar	alθár

30. Velar a. When immediately before **o** or **u**, when in contact with a following **g** or **x**, or when before l in a closed syllable, Spanish *a* may become velar. The tongue is drawn back a little more than for medial **a** and the back of it assumes a somewhat concave or hollow shape. This sound approaches the English *a* in *father*. The same symbol is used in this book for the velar **a** as for medial **a**.

EXAMPLES

causa	**káu̯sa**	hago	**ăgo**
autor	**au̯tó̦r**	cajón	**kaxó̦n**
ahogar	**aogár**	igual	**igwál**

BACK VOWELS

31. Closed o. Orthography o, phonetic symbol o. The tongue is drawn back. The back of the tongue is raised towards the soft palate and the tip touches the lower alveoles. The lips are rounded and protruded slightly, forming a small oval opening. See Figure 10. Spanish closed **o** is similar to English *o* in *tone*, but it is uniform throughout and does not end in a diphthongal glide. The muscular tension is quite pronounced.

FIG. 10. Closed o.

Spanish *o* is pronounced closed in open syllables. Exceptions are noted below.

EXAMPLES

todo	tóđo	decoro	dekóro
coma	kóma	hermoso	ęrmóso
sonar	sonár	oloroso	oloróso
asomó	asomó	no dijo	nó đíxo

32. Open o. Orthography o, phonetic symbol ǫ. In the pronunciation of open o the tongue position

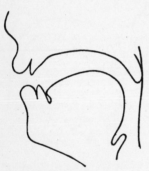

is in general as in closed o. The back of the tongue, however, is not raised so much towards the soft palate and the lips are wider open and less protruded. This sound is similar to English *o* in *gone*, although not so open. See Figure 11.

Fig. 11. Open ǫ.

Spanish *o* is pronounced ǫ in the following cases:

1. In closed syllables.
2. When in contact with trilled *r* (ř) anywhere.
3. When before the *j* sound (x).
4. In the diphthongs *oi, oy.*

EXAMPLES

compra	kǫmpra	corre	kǭr̄ę
contar	kǫntár	rosa	r̄ǫsa
hondos	ǫndǫs	hoja	ǫxa
cojo	kǫ́xo	robo	r̄ǫ́ƀo
veloz	belǫ́θ	ojos	ǫ́xǫs
perdón	pęrđǫ́n	oigo	ǫ́įgo
sol	sǫ́l	soy	sǫ́į

33. Closed u. Orthography u, phonetic symbol u. The tongue is drawn back. The back of the tongue is raised closely towards the soft palate, much more than for o, and the tip of the tongue is lowered to a position even with the lower alveoles. The lips are rounded and protruded much more than for o, and the oval-shaped opening is much smaller. See Figure 12. This Span-

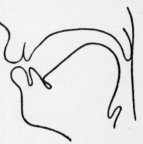

FIG. 12. Closed u.

ish vowel is similar to English u in *rule*, but it is uniform throughout and the muscular tension is quite pronounced.

Spanish *u* is pronounced closed in open syllables, and with the variation discussed below also in closed syllables.

Examples

puro	púro	único	úniko
curar	kurár	humilde	umílde
estudia	estúđja	pureza	puréθa
algunos	algúnọs	duración	duraθjón

34. Open u. In most closed syllables Spanish
u has a more open quality than the closed u described
above. The back of the tongue is raised towards
the soft palate to a position not quite as high as for
u, and the lips are rounded and protruded as for
closed o. This sound is between the closed Spanish
u and the English *u* of *put*. It is very difficult for
English-speaking students to pronounce Spanish
open u even approximately correctly. Experience
in attempting to teach this sound shows that the
tendency is to relapse into the more open sound of
English *put*. For these reasons this sound is represented by the same phonetic symbol as for closed
u. The teacher of Spanish, however, who is thoroughly familiar with this open sound of *u* in closed
syllables may very properly teach it. See §§ **24**
and **25.**

Examples

punto	púnto	suspender	suspendẹr
busca	búska	conjunción	kọŋxunθjọ́n
burla	búrla	estructura	estruktúra

For short and open *u* in the diphthongs, see § **36.**

35. Semiconsonantal u. Orthography u or hu, phonetic symbol w. The articulation is in general similar to that of closed u, but the sound is of shorter duration and the back of the tongue is raised so closely to the soft palate that a slight friction is produced. This sound is semiconsonantal and is similar to English *w* in *we*. See Figure 13.

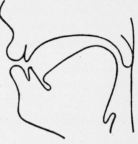

Fig. 13.   Semiconsonantal **w**.

The semiconsonantal sound of **w** is given to Spanish *u* or *hu* when immediately before a vowel with which it forms a syllable.

EXAMPLES

bueno	bwéno	acueducto	akweđúkto
puerta	pwẹrta	huérfano	wẹrfano
cuando	kwándo	hueso	wéso
abuelo	aƀwélo	muy	mwí
cuidar	kwiđár	Luis	lwís

When initial in a syllable in emphatic articulation the back of the tongue is raised to a position very close to the soft palate, and in popular pronunciation the result is the continuant or fricative consonant **g** + **w**. See § **70**.

Examples

huerta	gwę́rta
huevo	gwébo
ahuecar	agwekár

Diphthongs

36. The vowels *i*, *y*, and *u* combine with the strong vowels *a*, *e*, *o*, which they follow, to form the Spanish diphthongs. These are nine orthographically, but phonetically only six, since the *i* and *y* have the same sound here.

The Spanish diphthongs are :

ai, ay; au   ei, ey; eu   oi, oy; ou

In these diphthongs the strong vowels retain their full syllabic value while the weak vowels lose their syllabic value. The qualities of these strong vowels have been discussed already in the various sections that treat of the vowels. The vowel *a* is somewhat velar, § **30**, and the *e* and *o* are open, §§ **28, 32**. In the diphthongs **eu, ou**, however, the **e** and **o** are closed.

The final weak vowels *i*, *y*, and *u* of the diphthongs are pronounced open at the beginning of their articulation, somewhat like the open *i* (here also written *y*) and *u* described in §§ **25** and **34**, but they end as closed vowels, very short and with an almost imperceptible friction, although never as pronounced as in **j** and **w** of §§ **26** and **35**. These weak *i* and *u* sounds are called semivocalic. Their phonetic symbols are i̯ and u̯.

The Spanish diphthongs have the following approximately equivalent English diphthongal sounds:

ORTHOGRAPHY	PHONETIC SYMBOLS	APPROX. ENG. EQUIVALENTS
ai, ay	ai̯	*i* in *mine*
au	au̯	*ou* in *out*
ei, ey	ẹi̯	*a* in *fate*
eu	eu̯	
ou	ou̯	*o* in *note*

EXAMPLES

aire	ái̯re	ley	lẹ́i̯
bailar	bai̯lár	deuda	déu̯đa
hay	ái̯	oigo	ọ́i̯go
causa	káu̯sa	hoy	ọ́i̯
aceite	aθẹ́i̯te	bou	bóu̯

CHAPTER III

CONSONANTS

General Remarks

37. The distinction between vowels and consonants has been given in §§ **1–5**. A consonant may be defined as voiced or voiceless breath modified by the organs of speech above the larynx and with audible friction. Consonants, therefore, may be voiced or voiceless, that is, the vocal chords may or may not vibrate during their articulation. The distinction between voiced and voiceless consonants is fundamental and important, § **3**. But aside from this general, fundamental, and important division of consonants into voiced and voiceless, consonants are classified under two general divisions: first, according to the place of articulation, § **7**; and second, according to the manner of articulation, § **8**.

38. Classification of Spanish consonants according to the place of articulation. In the mouth cavity the various positions of the tongue, teeth, lips, etc., determine the articulation of speech-sounds. Classifying all the Spanish consonants according to the place of articulation, that is, according to the organs that articulate them, we have the following classes. As the student will see, the names themselves tell us what organs articulate them (but see § 7, end).

1. **Bilabials.** The organs of articulation are the lips : p, b, ƀ, m.

2. **Labiodentals.** The organs of articulation are the lower lip and the edges of the upper teeth : f, ṃ.

3. **Interdentals.** The organs of articulation are the tip or blade of the tongue and the edges of the upper teeth : θ, đ, ẓ.

4. **Dentals.** The organs of articulation are the tip of the tongue and the inner surface of the upper teeth : t, d.

5. **Alveolars.** The organs of articulation are the tip of the tongue and the alveoles or gum ridges of the upper teeth : s, z, n, l, r, r̄.

6. **Palatals.** The organs of articulation are the blade or front of the tongue and the hard palate : ḷ, ṇ, ĉ, ŷ, y, j.

7. **Velars.** The organs of articulation are the back of the tongue and the soft palate or uvula : k, g, ǥ, ŋ, x, w.

See Figures 1 and 14, and § **40.**

39. Classification of Spanish consonants according to the manner of articulation. Classifying the Spanish consonants according to the manner of

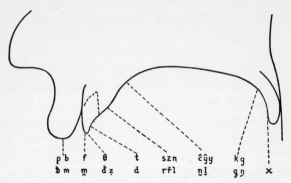

Fɪɢ. 14. Spanish consonants: Place of articulation.

articulation, that is, according to the manner in which the organs articulate them, we have the following classes:

1. **Explosives**, formed by a complete stoppage, that is, by completely closing the passage of the air and then suddenly removing the obstacle, or obstacles, allowing the air to escape producing an explosive sound: **p, b, t, d, k, g**.

2. **Semiexplosives**, formed by a complete but momentaneous stoppage, but removing the obstacle slowly and gently: **ĉ, ŷ**.

3. **Continuants** (called also **fricatives**), formed by a partial stoppage which allows the air to pass through a narrow passage, producing a continuous friction: **ƀ, f, θ, đ, ẓ, s, z, l, ḷ, y, j, g, x, w**.

Fricatives that are formed by the passing of the

air through the sides of the mouth are also called laterals: l, ḷ.

4. **Nasals**, formed by lowering the soft palate, so that the uvula shuts off the passage of the breath through the mouth and forces it to pass through the nose: m, ɱ, n, ṇ, ŋ.

5. **Vibrants**, formed by a vibration or a series of rapid vibrations of the tongue against the upper alveoles: r, r̄.

40. Table of Spanish consonants. A table of all the Spanish consonants classified according to the place and manner of articulation is given on page 34. The semiconsonants j and w are included, but not the consonantal variations due to assimilation or other accidental changes mentioned in § **76**. The letters are the phonetic symbols.

41. General character of the pronunciation of Spanish consonants. In studying the pronunciation of the Spanish consonants it is important to keep in mind the fact that in general Spanish consonants are articulated with greater muscular tension than in English, the result being a clearer and more distinct articulation. Although the muscular tension is greater when the consonant is near the accented or stressed syllable, the general consonantal weakening due to the weak muscular tension of the articulation, such as the weak pronunciation of English *t* which frequently becomes *d* in *put it,*

Place of Articulation →	Bilabials		Labio-dentals		Inter-dentals		Dentals		Alveolars		Palatals		Velars	
	Voiceless	Voiced	Voiceless	Voiced	Voiceless	Voiced	Voiceless	Voiced	Voiceless	Voiced	Voiceless	Voiced	Voiceless	Voiced
Explosives	p	b					t	d					k	g
Semi-explosives											ĉ	ŷ		
Continuants		ƀ	f		θ	đ ż			s	z		yj	x	gw
Laterals										l		ļ		
Nasals		m		ɱ						n		ņ		ŋ
Vibrants										r r̄				
													← Manner of Articulation	

Table of Spanish Consonants

34

let it, etc., is very rare in Spanish. This is in general
the character of the Spanish consonants as compared
with the English consonants. In the case of the
continuants ƀ, đ, g, however, the muscular tension
is less pronounced. These consonants are the
most characteristically Spanish in the whole range
of Spanish speech-sounds and their correct articulation is a source of much trouble to English-speaking
students. The complete mastery of them is almost
impossible to a foreigner, but a close study of their
place and manner of articulation together with
continual practice with the aid of the teacher will
result in fair accuracy in their pronunciation.

**42. The voiceless explosives compared with their
English equivalents.** In the articulation of the
voiceless explosives p, t, k it is very important to
know that the Spanish consonants are pure explosives
and not aspirated explosives. In English these
consonants are usually pronounced with audible
breathing, especially in the initial position. The
difference in the articulation of the Spanish pure
explosives and the English aspirated explosives
is to be found in the fact that in Spanish the voiceless explosives are articulated with a weak momen-
tary explosion that is followed immediately by the
vibrations of the vocal chords in anticipation of
the ensuing vowel, padre **páđre**, tapa **tápa**, casa
kása, whereas in English voice, or the vibrations

of the vocal chords, begins much later and the explosion is stronger and accompanied by an audible voiceless breathing similar to a weak *h* sound. In the articulation of such words as *past, task, car* the initial consonant is really followed by a weakly aspirated *h* sound, *pʰast, tʰask, cʰar*. This aspiration should be carefully avoided in Spanish.

43. Silent h. The letter *h* is silent in modern Spanish: hoja ǫxa, ahora aǫra.[1]

BILABIAL AND LABIODENTAL CONSONANTS

44. Voiceless explosive p. Orthography p, phonetic symbol p. Spanish *p* is a voiceless bilabial explosive similar to English *p*. The explosion, however, is weaker, and there is no aspiration. See § 42. See Figure 15.

EXAMPLES

parte	**párte**	culpa	**kúlpa**
papel	**papél**	cuerpo	**kwérpo**

45. Voiced explosive b. Orthography b, v, phonetic symbol b. The letters *b* and *v* are pronounced alike in Spanish, although orthographically they are not interchangeable. Each has two different

[1] Contrary to § 31 this word is usually pronounced aǫra, with open o, but in slow, emphatic pronunciation aora, with closed o, is also heard.

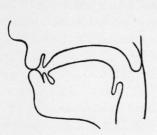

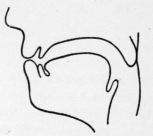

Fig. 15. The explosives p, b.   Fig. 16. Continuant ƀ.

sounds, a voiced explosive sound, and a voiced continuant or fricative sound.

When initial in a phonic or breath group (see § 10 b, note) or when after **m** or **n** (phonetically also **m**), whether within a word or between words, *b* (or *v*) is a voiced bilabial explosive similar to English *b* in *boy*, but less strong.   See Figure 15.

EXAMPLES

buenos días	**bwénọz días**	sín vida	**sim bída**
¡ basta !	**básta**	han venido	**ám benído**
vámonos	**bámonọs**	un vaso	**úm báso**
hombre	**ọ́mbre**	en balde	**em bálde**
invierno	**imbjẹ́rno**	un vapor	**úm bapọ́r**

46. Voiced continuant b. Orthography b, v, phonetic symbol ƀ.   In all other positions, that is, when not initial in a phonic or breath group and when not after *m* or *n*, Spanish *b* (or *v*) is a voiced bilabial continuant or fricative, a sound not found in English. The lips do not close completely as in § 45, but allow the breath to pass between them through a very narrow passage as in the position that the lips obtain in blowing. The distance between the lips is from one to two millimeters. See Figure 16. Between vowels the muscular tension is especially weak and the articulation rapid.

EXAMPLES

no vamos	nó ƀámọs	lobo	lóƀo
eso basta	éso ƀásta	sobre	sóƀre
mi vaso	mi ƀáso	objeto	ọƀxéto
hablaba	aƀláƀa	por ver	pọr ƀẹr
es verdad	éz ƀẹrđáđ	abrigo	aƀrígo

47. Voiced bilabial nasal m. Orthography m, n, phonetic symbol m. Spanish *m* is a voiced bilabial nasal similar to English *m* in *more*. The velum is

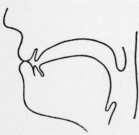

open and the breath passes both through the mouth and the nose. See Figure 17.

When immediately before the bilabial consonants *p*, *b*, *v*, the consonant *n* is also pronounced **m**. See § 45.

Fɪɢ. 17. Bilabial nasal m.

EXAMPLES

cama	káma	ambiguo	ambígwo
tiempo	tjémpo	sin par	sim pár
hombre	ǫmbre	invierno	imbięrno

As final in a word *m* occurs in a few learned or foreign words and it is then pronounced n: ultimatum **ultimátun**, álbum **álƀun**, Abraham **aƀrán**.

48. Voiceless labiodental continuant f. Orthography f, phonetic symbol f. Spanish *f* is a voiceless labiodental continuant, the lower lip touching the edges of the upper front teeth. It is similar to English *f*. See Figure 18.

EXAMPLES

fueron	fwérǫn	ofrecer	ofreθęr
familia	famílja	perfecto	pęrfękto
flaco	fláko	esfuerzo	esfwęrθo

49. Labiodental n. Orthography n, phonetic symbol m̩. When the consonant *n* comes immedi-

FIG. 18. Labiodental f.

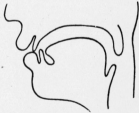

FIG. 19. Labiodental m̩.

ately before an *f* it is a voiced labiodental nasal. The place of articulation is as in **f**, § **48**, but the manner of articulation is as in **m**, § **47**. The breath passes through the nose and often the ṃ disappears completely, leaving the preceding vowel nasalized. See Figure 19.

EXAMPLES

enfermo	eṃférmo	confiesa	koṃfjésa
un favor	úṃ faḅọr	enfadar	eṃfađár

DENTAL AND INTERDENTAL CONSONANTS

50. Voiceless explosive t. Orthography t, phonetic symbol t. Spanish *t* is a voiceless dental explosive. The tip of the tongue touches the inner surface of the upper front teeth and in emphatic pronunciation reaches as far as the alveoles. The sides of the tongue touch the upper molars. See Figures 20 and 21. Spanish *t* is similar to English *t*, but English *t* is alveolar and not dental. It is also important to remember that Spanish *t* is a pure explosive and not accompanied by audible breathing as is the case with English *t*. See § **42**.

EXAMPLES

toma	tóma	pintar	pintár
tinta	tínta	estáte	estáte
tarde	tárđe	patio	pátjo
tres	trés	cuatro	kwátro

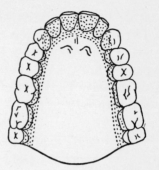

Fig. 20. Explosives t, d. Fig. 21. Explosives t, d.

51. Voiced explosive d. Orthography d, phonetic symbol d. Spanish *d* has two sounds, a voiced explosive sound and a voiced continuant or fricative sound.

When initial in a phonic group or when after *n* or *l*, whether within a word or between words, Spanish *d* is a voiced dental explosive; place of articulation as in *t*, § **50**. See Figures 20 and 21. It is similar to English *d*, but dental, not alveolar.

Examples

dame	dáme	aldea	aldéa
donde	dǫnde	mundo	múndo
falda	fálda	sin dar	sin dár
con dos	kǫn dǫs	al dar	al dár
el día	ęl día	un día	ún día

52. Voiced continuant d. Orthography d, phonetic symbol đ. In all other positions, that is, when not initial in a phonic group and when not after *n* or *l*, and conspicuously between vowels,

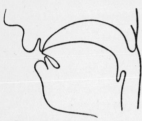

Spanish *d* is a voiced interdental continuant similar to English *th* in *this*, but much weaker and less interdental. The tip of the tongue touches the edges of the upper front teeth very gently. The tongue movement is very rapid and the contact very brief, the breath escaping between the tip of the tongue and the edges of the teeth with a continuous, gentle friction much less pronounced than in the English *th* in *this*. The Spanish sound that is almost an exact equivalent of the English *th* in *this* is the consonant *z* when before a voiced consonant. See § **56.** See Figure 22.

Fig. 22. Continuant đ.

EXAMPLES

admirar	ađmirár	le doy	le đó̦i̦
adjetivo	ađxetíbo	su día	su đía
verde	bér̦đe	ha dicho	a đíĉo
padre	páđre	los dos	lo̦z đó̦s
medida	međíđa	por dar	po̦r đár

53. The pronunciation of d in the ending –ado.
In slow and careful pronunciation the *d* in this ending
is regularly pronounced as a continuant in the
same way as any other intervocalic *d*, according to
§ 52. But ordinarily, in careless, familiar conversation, it is very weakly articulated and often altogether silent. A systematic regularity in the
pronunciation of đ in this termination as a clear continuant in familiar conversation would certainly be
looked upon as pedantic and affected, but to omit it
altogether regularly would be considered incorrect.
English-speaking students would do well to articulate
đ in this termination very weakly, the tip of the
tongue moving rapidly in the direction of the edges
of the upper teeth but without really touching them.

EXAMPLES

ORTHOGRAPHY	CAREFUL PRONUNCIATION	FAMILIAR PRONUNCIATION
estado	estáđo	estáo
comprado	kọmpráđo	kọmpráo
abogado	abogáđo	abogáo

54. Pronunciation of final d. When *d* is final
in a word but followed immediately by the vowel
or consonant of another word in the same phonic
group it is pronounced continuant đ : su bondad es
infinita, su bọndađ es iṃfiníta, la edad media la
eđáđ méđja, llamadlos ḷamáđlọs. But when *d*

is absolutely final before a pause it is pronounced very weakly and partly unvoiced. In some parts of Castile and among the lower classes of Madrid this sound becomes completely voiceless, practically the same as voiceless interdental θ, § 55.

But final *d* is treated also in another manner. In the majority of nouns that end in *d*, whether within a phonic group or in the absolute final position before a pause, *d* may be silent altogether: usted usté, verdad bẹrđá, mitad mitá, atrocidad atroθiđá. Most educated people, however, attempt to pronounce at least a weak final đ in all the above cases.

In the phonetic texts and exercises used in this book all the varieties of continuant đ treated above as well as in § 53 are represented by the same symbol, continuant đ, which is a close enough approximation to all for the beginner. It should be pronounced very weakly when intervocalic or final.

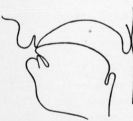

FIG. 23. Interdental θ.

55. Voiceless interdental continuant z or c (e, i). Orthography z, c, phonetic symbol θ. Spanish *z* in all cases, and also *c* when before *e* or *i*, is a voiceless interdental continuant, similar to English *th* in *thin*. The tip of the tongue moves forward between the teeth more than in continuant đ, touching gently the upper front teeth. The lower surface of the tip of the tongue rests on the lower teeth. See Figure 23.

EXAMPLES

hacer	aθḗr	cruz	krúθ
cinco	θíŋko	razón	řaθǫ́n
zorra	θǫ́řa	ceniza	θeníθa

56. Voiced interdental continuant z. Orthography z, phonetic symbol ẓ. When z is final in a syllable before a voiced consonant, it becomes partially or completely voiced, the result being a sound resembling the English th in this or a strongly articulated Spanish continuant đ.

EXAMPLES

| juzgar | xuzgár | en vez de | em bḗẓ đe |
| hallazgo | aḷáẓgo | voz de niño | bǫ́ẓ đe níṇo |

ALVEOLAR CONSONANTS

57. Voiceless alveolar s. Orthography s, phonetic symbol s. Spanish s has two sounds, a voiceless alveolar continuant sound, which is the normal sound, and a voiced alveolar continuant, which occurs only when before a voiced consonant.

In the articulation of normal voiceless s the tip of the tongue touches the alveoles of the upper

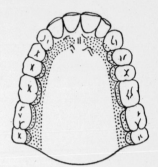

FIG. 24. Alveolar s. FIG. 25. Alveolar s.

front teeth while the sides of the tongue rest on both sides of the mouth against the inner surface of the upper molars. The middle of the tongue assumes a somewhat concave form. See Figures 24 and 25. Spanish voiceless *s* is quite different from English *s*, which is dental rather than alveolar. It should also be noted that in English it is the blade and not the tip of the tongue that reaches towards the alveoles and that the tip rests on the lower front teeth. In some regions of Castile this alveolar *s* is articulated even higher, the result being almost a front palatal *s*.

EXAMPLES

saber	saβẹr	siempre	sjémpre
solos	sólọs	despacio	despáθjo
salas	sálas	estás	estás

58. Voiced alveolar s. Orthography s, phonetic symbol z. Spanish *s* is voiced when final in a syllable and immediately before a voiced consonant. This sound is exactly the same as alveolar *s*, but voiced. It is different from English *s* in *rose* in the same way that voiceless *s* is different from English voiceless *s* in *case*.

EXAMPLES

esbelto	ezbélto	las botas	laz bótas
es de él	éz đél	los lados	loz láđos
desde	dézđe	es verdad	éz berđáđ
rasgo	řázgo	las manos	laz mános

59. Alveolar nasal n. Orthography n, phonetic symbol n. Spanish *n* has four different sounds:

1. When immediately before a bilabial consonant it is pronounced m, § 47: en paz em páθ, envidia embíđja, un vaso úm báso.

2. When immediately before *f* it is a labiodental ɱ, § 49: enfermo eɱférmo, confío koɱfío, en fin eɱ fín.

3. When final in a syllable and immediately before a velar consonant it is a velar nasal ŋ, § 73: tengo téŋgo, banco báŋko, sin ganas siŋ gánas, con jota koŋ xóta.

4. In all cases not included above, that is, when initial in a syllable, when between vowels, or when before any consonant except bilabials, velars, or *f*,

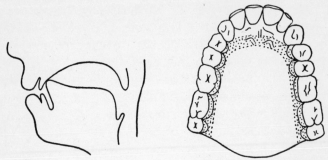

FIG. 26.   Alveolar n.   FIG. 27.   Alveolar n.

Spanish *n* is a voiced alveolar nasal.   The tip of the tongue touches the upper alveoles or gums while the sides of the tongue touch the inner surface of the upper molars, as in *s*.   The breath passes through the nose.   See Figures 26 and 27.   English pure *n* is pronounced even higher than Spanish *n*.   Spanish *n* is alveolar; English *n* is often post-alveolar.

EXAMPLES

nada	**náđa**	junio	**xúnjo**
carne	**kárne**	enano	**enáno**
himno	**ímno**	piensa	**pjénsa**

In the prefixes *ins*, *cons*, *trans*, the *n* is pronounced very weak.   In familiar conversation the *n* in these prefixes is sometimes silent, leaving the preceding vowel slightly nasalized.

60. Voiced lateral l. Orthography l, phonetic symbol l. Spanish *l* is a voiced, alveolar, lateral continuant. The tip of the tongue touches the alveoles or gums of the upper teeth, as in *n*, § 59, while the breath passes around the sides of the tongue, producing a slight friction. See Figure 28. Spanish *l* is different from English *l* in that it is a uniform sound throughout, whereas in English many varieties of *l* are formed. In English the tip of the

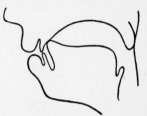

Fig. 28.   Alveolar l.

tongue touches also the upper alveoles or gums, but the main part of the tongue is free to take up any vowel position. In most cases English *l* is articulated not only by the tip of the tongue touching the alveoles of the upper front teeth, but also by the back of the tongue being raised toward the palate. This last tongue movement should be avoided in the articulation of Spanish *l*.

EXAMPLES

lana	lána	olvida	ǫlƀíđa
pelo	pélo	habla	áƀla
clavo	klaƀo	papel	papél

61. Simple r. Orthography r, phonetic symbol r. Spanish *r* has two sounds:

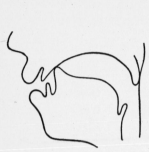

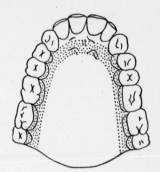

Fig. 29.   Simple **r**.   Fig. 30.   Simple **r**.

1. When not initial in a word and when not preceded by *l*, *n*, or *s* it is a simple vibrant, **r**.

2. When initial in a word, when after *l*, *n*, or *s*, and when doubled (**rr**), it is a multiple vibrant, **r̄**.

Simple **r** is a voiced, alveolar, single vibrant sound. The sides of the tongue rest on the gums and inner surface of the upper molars, stopping the passage of the breath through the sides of the mouth. At the same time the tip of the tongue is raised quickly and its edges touch the upper alveoles in a single vibration or flip of the tongue. Simultaneously the tongue is drawn back and its middle assumes a concave shape. See Figures 29 and 30. Spanish simple **r** is quite different from either the British or American English *r*. In American English the tip of the tongue is turned back against the front palate, the tongue assumes a more concave shape, and the resulting sound, a more open, more vocalic, and longer *r*, is not even an approximation to Spanish *r*.

EXAMPLES

para	pára	siempre	sjémpre
seré	seré	fuerte	fwẹrte
arder	arḍẹr	trigo	trígo
corto	kọrto	quiero	kjéro

In the pronunciation of the Spanish groups voiceless consonant + *r* English-speaking students should articulate each consonant with its clear and pure quality and not a voiceless consonant + aspiration + *r*, as is the case in English: creo **kréo**, presto **présto**, tres **trés**.

62. Multiple or trilled r. Orthography r, rr, phonetic symbol r̄. When initial in a word, when after *l*, *n*, or *s*, and when doubled, Spanish *r* is a voiced, alveolar, multiple vibrant sound. The place and manner of articulation are in general as in simple **r**, § **61**. But, the tip of the tongue is raised so that the edges touch the uppermost part of the alveoles, striking against the alveoles, not with a single flip or vibration, but with several very rapid vibrations. Trilled *r* has usually from two to five vibrations, and in emphatic speech the number of vibrations may be even more than five. The muscular tension is greater than in simple **r** and the tongue contact

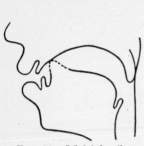

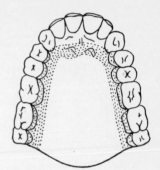

Fig. 31. Multiple vibrant
or trilled r̄.

Fig. 32. Multiple vibrant
or trilled r̄.

both at the tip and at the sides against the alveoles and inner surface of the upper molars much more pronounced. See Figures 31 and 32.

Examples

rey	r̄éi̦	enredo	enr̄é̦đo	carro	kár̄o̦
rico	r̄íko	honra	ó̦nr̄a	tierra	tjé̦r̄a
ruido	r̄wíđo	alrededor	alr̄e̦đe̦đó̦r	correr	ko̦r̄é̦r

Palatal and Velar Consonants

63. Continuant y. Orthography y, hi, phonetic symbol y. The sound of Spanish *y* or *hi* when initial in a syllable is usually a voiced palatal continuant or fricative. The tongue position is similar to that which produces the vowel i, § 24, and the semiconsonant j, § 26, but the tongue is raised much higher. The tip of the tongue rests on the

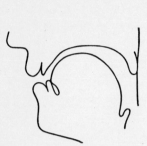
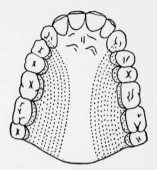

Fig. 33. Continuant **y**.   Fig. 34. Continuant **y**.

lower front teeth and the front and middle of the
tongue are raised in a convex shape closely toward
the hard palate, touching it over a wide area on
both sides of the mouth. The breath passes through
a narrow opening in the middle of the mouth, producing a strong friction. See Figures 33 and 34.
Continuant **y** is a stronger palatal friction than
English *y* in *yes*. This English sound is more like
Spanish semiconsonantal **j** of § **26**.

EXAMPLES

yelmo	yę́lmo	ayuda	ayúđa	hierro	yę́r̄o
ya	yá	leyes	léyes	hierba	yę́rɓa
yo	yó	y eso	yéso	hielo	yélo
ayer	ayę́r	y a él	ya ę́l	se hiere	se yére

**64. Semiexplosive y. Orthography y, hi, phonetic
symbol ŷ.** Continuant **y** of § **63** is in general the

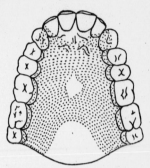

FIG. 35. Semiexplosive ŷ.   FIG. 36. Semiexplosive ŷ.

sound of Spanish initial *y* or *hi*. However, when
immediately after *l* or *n*, or when pronounced very
emphatically in the accented position, the tongue
may be raised so as to form a complete contact
with the hard palate over a wide area. The result
is a voiced palatal semiexplosive, ŷ. See Figures
35 and 36. This *y* sound is similar to English *g* in
gem.

Beginners in Spanish are advised to pronounce
Spanish initial *y* or *hi* as continuant *y* in all cases,
except when immediately after *l* or *n*, where the
semiexplosive ŷ sound is more commonly heard.

EXAMPLES

inyectar	inŷ̧ektár	el hielo	ęl ŷélo
cónyuge	kǫnŷuxe	con hierro	kǫn ŷę́ṟǫ
un yugo	ún ŷúgo	sin hierbas	sin ŷę́rƀas

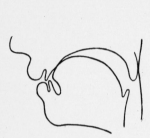

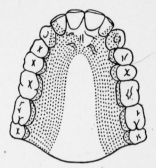

Fig. 37. Semiexplosive ĉ.   Fig. 38. Semiexplosive ĉ.

65. Semiexplosive ch.   Orthography ch, phonetic symbol ĉ. The Spanish digraph *ch* represents a single sound, a voiceless, prepalatal semiexplosive, ĉ. The front of the tongue is raised against the alveoles of the upper front teeth and the front palate, making a momentaneous but complete stoppage. On the sides of the mouth the tongue contact covers a wide area from the molars to the sides of the palate. Finally the front of the tongue is removed slowly from the alveoles and front palate and the breath escapes between the narrow passage thus formed, producing a slight friction. This sound is very similar to English *ch* in *cheer*. See Figures 37 and 38.

EXAMPLES

mucho	múĉo	muchacho	muĉáĉo
leche	léĉe	chico	ĉíko
hacha	áĉa	chasco	ĉásko

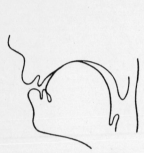 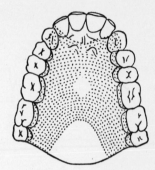

FIG. 39. Palatal ɲ.   FIG. 40. Palatal ɲ.

66. Palatal nasal ñ. Orthography ñ, phonetic symbol ɲ. Spanish ñ is a voiced palatal nasal, ɲ. The middle of the tongue is raised against the hard palate, making a complete stoppage, while the tip of the tongue rests on the lower front teeth. Since the tongue shuts off completely the passage of the breath through the mouth it passes through the nose. With the exception of its nasal quality the articulation of this sound is in general the same as semiexplosive ŷ. See Figures 39 and 40. Spanish ɲ is a single and uniform sound and not a double sound, such as English *n* + *i* in *onion*.

EXAMPLES

año	áɲo	pequeño	pekéɲo
leña	léɲa	cariño	karíɲo
paño	páɲo	enseñar	enseɲár

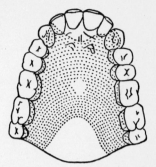

Fig. 41. Palatal ļ.   Fig. 42. Palatal ļ.

67. Lateral palatal ll. Orthography ll, phonetic symbol ļ. Spanish *ll* is a voiced, lateral palatal, ļ. The middle of the tongue is raised as in the case of ŷ and ņ against the hard palate over a wide area. On both sides of the mouth, by the back molars, the tongue forms two narrow passages through which the breath passes, producing the lateral frictions. See Figures 41 and 42. Spanish ļ is a single and uniform sound and not a double sound, such as English *ll* + *i* in *million*, a sound group almost the equivalent of Spanish *l* + *i* in aliado **aljáđo**, escolio **eskóljo**.

EXAMPLES

ellos	éļọs	llave	ļábe
halla	áļa	llega	ļéga
caballo	kabáļo	llamar	ļamár
estrella	estréļa	llueve,	ļwébe

68. The velar consonants c, q, k. Orthography c (when before a, o, u or before a consonant), qu, k, phonetic symbol k. The sound of Spanish *c* when before *a, o, u* or before a consonant, of the

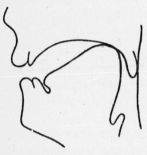

digraph *qu*, and of *k* is a voiceless velar explosive, **k**. The back of the tongue is raised against the soft palate, making a complete stoppage, and then suddenly removed. The sound is similar to English *k*, but there is no aspiration. See §§ **42** and **44**. In the articulations ka, ko, ku, kw, i.e. before the back vowels, the point of contact of the back of the tongue is with the soft palate. See Figure 43. In the articulations ke, ki, kj, i.e. before the front vowels, however, the point of contact is between the soft palate and the back of the hard palate.

FIG. 43. Velar explosives k, g.

EXAMPLES

capa	kápa	efecto	efékto
como	kómo	quepa	képa
cuerpo	kwérpo	aquí	akí
tocar	tokár	quien	kjén
doctor	doktór	kilogramo	kilográmo

69. Voiced velar explosive g. Orthography g, gu, phonetic symbol g. Spanish *g* has three sounds :

1. When before *a*, *o*, or *u* or before a consonant, or when before *e* or *i* in the groups *gue*, *gui*, and in all these cases when initial in a phonic group, or when after *n*, it is a voiced velar explosive, g.

2. In all other cases, except when immediately before *e* or *i* in the groups *ge*, *gi*, it is a voiced velar continuant, **g**, § **70**.

3. When immediately before *e* or *i* in the groups *ge*, *gi*, it is a voiceless velar or uvular continuant, x, § **72**.

When immediately before *a*, *o*, or *u* or before a consonant, or when before *e* or *i* in the groups *gue*, *gui* (the *u* being silent here), and in all cases when initial in a phonic group, or when after *n* anywhere, Spanish *g* is a voiced velar explosive, g. The place and manner of articulation are exactly as in k, see Figure 43, but the sound is voiced instead of voiceless. Before *e* or *i* in the groups *gue*, *gui* the point of contact is also farther to the front, as in **ke, ki, kj.** In general the sound is similar to English *g* in *go* and *get*.

EXAMPLES

gana	gána	sin ganas	siŋ gánas
goma	góma	engaño	eŋgáɲo
guerra	gẹ́r̃a	tengo	téŋgo
grande	gránde	sangre	sáŋgre

70. Voiced velar continuant g. Orthography g, gu, phonetic symbol g. When not initial in a phonic group, when not after *n*, and when not immediately before *e* or *i* in the groups *ge*, *gi*, Spanish *g* is a voiced velar continuant, **g**. The articulation

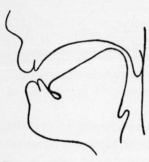

of this sound is in general the same as explosive **g**, but the back of the tongue does not form a complete contact with the soft palate and the breath passes through the narrow passage, producing a slight, continuous friction. See Figure 44. Continuant **g** has the same relation to explosive g

FIG. 44. Velar continuant **g**.

that continuants **ƀ** and **đ**, §§ **46** and **52**, have to explosives **b** and **d**, §§ **45** and **51**. In the intervocalic position continuant **g** is very weakly pronounced, the tongue being lower than in the ordinary position and the passage between the tongue and the soft palate much wider. See also § 46.

EXAMPLES

agua	**ágwa**	rogar	**r̦ogár**
siglo	**síglo**	hago	**ágo**
sagrado	**sagráđo**	por ganar	**por ganár**
digno	**dígno**	la guerra	**la gę́r̦a**

In the groups *cc* and *cn* the ordinary pronunciation of the **k** sound in careful and emphatic articulation is as a velar explosive **k**: lección lękθjǫ́n, acción akθjǫ́n, técnica tę́knika; but in familiar conversation it is ordinarily pronounced as continuant **g**: lęgθjǫ́n, agθjǫ́n, tę́gnika.

71. Pronunciation of the letter x. The letter *x* is pronounced in Spanish in various ways. Historically *x* is equivalent to **ks** and it is so pronounced sometimes in learned, almost affected, pronunciation. In familiar conversation, however, it is treated in the following manner:

1. Before a consonant it is pronounced **s**: extraño estráṇo, exponer espoņę́r, explicar esplikár, exclamar esklamár.

2. Between vowels it is pronounced **gs**: examen ęgsámen, existe ęgsíste, éxito ę́gsito, exhibición ęgsibiθjǫ́n.

3. In some words *x* may be also pronounced **s**, even when between vowels: exacto esákto, auxilio aųsíljo, ausiliar aųsiljár.

72. Velar continuant j. Orthography j, g, phonetic symbol x. Spanish *j* in all positions, and *g* when immediately before *e* or *i*, is a voiceless velar continuant, **x**. The position of the tongue is in general as in **g**, § **70**, but the back of the tongue is raised to a position a little lower, towards the end of the soft palate, and the breath passes through

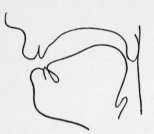

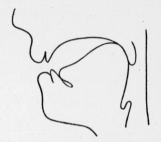

FIG. 45. Velar continuant x.   FIG. 46. Velar ŋ.

the narrow passage, producing a strong friction.
See Figure 45. Before the vowels *a, o, u* it is really
uvular instead of velar, the friction being produced
between the back of the tongue and the uvula.
It is distinguished also from **g** in that it is voiceless
instead of voiced. Spanish *x* is quite different from
English *h*, which is merely a weak pharyngeal
aspiration.

EXAMPLES

Juan	xwán	juez	xwé̦θ
hijo	íxo	gesto	xésto
rojo	r̄ó̦xo	fingir	fiŋxír
caja	káxa	gitano	xitáno

**73. Velar n. Orthography n, phonetic symbol
ŋ.** The various sounds of *n* have been treated in
§ 59.

When *n* comes before a velar consonant, whether
within a word or between words, it is a voiced velar

nasal, ŋ. The tongue takes the position of the velar consonant that follows, that is, it is raised against the soft palate in anticipation of the velar consonant. The result is a velar *n* similar to English *ng* in *sing*. See Figure 46.

EXAMPLES

tengo	téŋgo	en casa	eŋ kása
cinco	θíŋko	con ganas	koŋ gánas
ángel	áŋxęl	un carro	úŋ kár̬ǫ
lengua	léŋgwa	son cosas	sǫ́ŋ kósas

SILENT CONSONANTS

74. Silent consonants are rare in Spanish. In familiar conversation there is a tendency to drop intervocalic *d* in many words, especially in the termination *–ado*, § 53, and when final, § 54. We are now concerned with consonants that are regularly dropped in standard pronunciation.

1. The consonant *b* is often written but never pronounced in the words obscuro, subscribir, substraer, substituir, and their derivatives: ǫskúro, suskribír, sustraę́r, etc.

2. The consonant *j* is silent in reloj r̬ęló, but pronounced in the plural relojes r̬ęlóxes.

3. The consonant *p* is silent in psicología, pseudo, and their derivatives; in séptimo, septiembre,

subscriptor, and subscripción: **sikoloxía, séu̧đo, sétimo, setjémbre, suskritǫr,** etc.

4. The consonant *t* is silent in istmo **ízmo.**

5. In the word *usted*, final *d* is regularly silent in familiar conversation, and in poetry it is written without the *d* when the poet wishes to use synalepha, or for rhyme.

6. For silent *h*, see § **43.**

CHAPTER IV

SOUND CHANGES

ASSIMILATION

75. When two or more sounds are pronounced together in a phonic group many changes and modifications may take place, due for the most part to the phonetic laws of assimilation (tendency of neighboring unlike sounds to become alike) and dissimilation (tendency of neighboring like sounds to become unlike). We have already seen, for example, how the consonant n which is ordinarily an alveolar nasal, § **59**, becomes m when before a bilabial consonant, § **47**, the labiodental ɱ when before f, § **49**, and the velar nasal ŋ when before a velar consonant, § **73**. There are many other modifications and changes which may take place and which must be taken into consideration ; but they are not important enough to be represented in this book by special phonetic symbols. Among the most important of these minor changes are the following :

1. The consonants *n* and *l* when immediately before the interdental θ are not pronounced as alveolars, §§ **59**, **60**, but become interdentals owing

to assimilation to θ: encima enθíma, esperanza esperánθa, alzar alθár, el zapato ẹl θapáto.

2. The consonant s when immediately before θ, t, is not a voiceless alveolar, § 57, but a voiceless dental by assimilation : escena esθéna, pasta pásta.

3. The consonant s when immediately before đ is not always a voiced alveolar, § 58, but may become a voiced dental by assimilation to the đ: los dos lọz đọs, desde đézđe.

4. The consonant s when before r̄ is not a pure voiced alveolar continuant, but a sort of weak continuant r due to assimilation to r̄: es rico éz r̄íko, las ruedas laz r̄wéđas.

5. When two like consonants come together between words there is usually only one consonantal articulation, but a rather long one and distributed between the two syllables to which the consonants belong. Examples: edad dichosa eđáđ-điĉósa, el lobo ẹl-lóƀo, un niño ún-níọo, los sacos lọs-sákọs.

But there are other sound changes which the student must understand well before attempting to read or speak Spanish correctly in connected words and phrases. These changes may be studied under the two following divisions :

1. Liaison or linking of consonant + vowel between words.

2. Synalepha or the union of two or more vowels between words in one syllable.

LIAISON OR LINKING OF CONSONANT + VOWEL

76. When orthographic and phonetic syllabication are at variance we must follow phonetic syllabication in the study of phonetics. See §§ 10 and 16. In Spanish, therefore, a single consonant between vowels always goes with the following syllable, § 9 a : a-bo-rí-ge-nes, li-te-ra-tu-ra, i-no-por-tu-no, bie-nes-tar, ma-les-tar, no-so-tros, i-nhu-ma-no.

This same phonetic law which applies to an intervocalic consonant within a word is also applied to an intervocalic consonant between words. Therefore, within a phonic group the final consonant of a word is carried over or linked with the initial vowel of the following word with which it forms phonetically a syllable. See § 10. The consonant itself does not change here, but the preceding vowel may change since a final closed syllable has lost its final consonant and has therefore become open. In most of these cases vowels that were previously open become closed.

EXAMPLES

el hombre	e-lǫm-bre	con el otro	ko-ne-ló-tro
los ojos	lo-sǫ-xǫs	por el hijo	po-re-lí-xo
por eso	po-ré-so	es en eso	é-se-né-so
del otro	de-ló-tro	es al amo	é-sa-lá-mo
mal hice	má-lí-θe	dos han ido	dó-sá-ní-đo

Words and phrases of different meanings and of different spelling may have, therefore, exactly the same pronunciation :

el hado, helado	e-lá-đo
en ojo, enojo	e-nǫ-xo
las aves, la sabes	la-sá-ƀes
el hecho, helecho	e-lé-ĉo
el hijo, elijo	e-lí-xo

77. Linking of final y. In the case of final *y* between words the rule is not absolute. It may remain, forming a diphthong with the preceding vowel according to § 36, or it may be carried over and linked with the initial vowel of the following syllable, and pronounced continuant **y**.

EXAMPLES

la ley era	la lḕi̯ éra	*or*	la lé-yé-ra
soy así	sǫ́i̯ así	*or*	só-ya-sí
voy a ver	ƀǫ́i̯ a ƀẹ́r	*or*	ƀó-ya-ƀẹ́r
hay algo	ái̯ álgo	*or*	á-yál-go

78. Pronunciation of the conjunction y. The conjunction **y** may also be linked to the preceding vowel, forming a diphthong with it, or it may be linked with the initial vowel of the word that follows, as in the case of final **y**, § 77. In general the rules that govern the correct pronunciation of the conjunction **y** are the following :

1. When initial in a phonic group before a consonant, or when between consonants anywhere it is pronounced i: y se fué i se fwé, dos y dos dós i đǫs, los lunes y los martes lǫz lúnes i lǫz mártes.

2. When initial in a phonic group before a vowel it is linked with it and is pronounced continuant y, as in § 77: y era muy rico yéra mwí r̄íko, este y aquel éste yakę́l, y aunque venga yáy̨ ke b̄éŋga, treinta y uno tręį́nta yúno.

3. Between a consonant and a vowel within a phonic group it is pronounced semiconsonantal j, as in § 26: diez y ocho djeθjôĉo, dientes largos y afilados djéntez lárgo zjafiláđǫs.

NOTE. — If there is a pause after the consonant the conjunction *y* is no longer within a phonic group, but initial in a phonic group before a vowel, as in § 78, 2: dientes largos y afilados djéntez lárgǫs yafiláđǫs.

4. Between a vowel and a consonant it is pronounced semivocalic weak į̄ and forms a diphthong with the vowel that precedes it: padre y madre páđrę́į̄ máđre, esto y lo demás éstǫį̄ lo đemás, esa y la otra ésaį̨ la ótra, treinta y seis tręį́ntaį̨ sę́į̨s.

SYNALEPHA

79. When a word that ends in a vowel is followed by a word that begins with a vowel, between these vowels there may occur hiatus or synalepha. Hiatus occurs when each one of the vowels of the separate

words is pronounced with its full vocalic value and clear quality, each forming a separate syllable: tú eres **tú éres**, la hija la íxa. Synalepha occurs when the vowel that ends a word and the vowel that begins the following word are united into a single syllable: me ha dicho **me a͡ ɗíĉo**, uno estaba entero ú͡no está͡ɓa entéro, eso era así éso é͡ra así.

In very slow pronunciation and especially when the words in question are emphatically pronounced for contrast or to call special attention to them, or when the words are at the end of a stress group or at the end of a verse of poetry, hiatus may occur, but in ordinary conversation and in poetry it is extremely rare. In general it may be said that in most cases of contiguous vowels between words synalepha is the rule. It is of such frequent occurrence in Spanish that an elementary knowledge of the principal rules that govern its application is absolutely necessary if one is to learn to read and speak Spanish correctly and intelligently. The principal and elementary rules are the following.

80. When two [1] like vowels of different words come together within a phonic group contraction occurs and there is only one vowel pronounced.

---

[1] We say two vowels for the sake of simplicity. As a matter of fact there may be three or even four vowels joined together in one syllable to form synalepha. In the second example of § **80** there are three like vowels that are contracted into one.

Examples

quiere entrar	kjére entrár
no va a hacer nada	nó ƀá a aθę̊r náđa
habla antes que tú	áƀla ántes ke tú
yo os he dicho	yó os é đíĉo

81. When unlike vowels come together and both are strong vowels they are pronounced together in one syllable, each losing a little of its full vocalic character. The vowel *e* of the monosyllables *de, le, me, te, que, se, en, el*, is especially weak before or after an accented vowel. And in most cases when one of the vowels in question is accented that vowel bears the stress and retains more of its original, full quality. The vowel *a*, however, especially the preposition *a*, has a strong tendency to attract the accent.

Examples

todo estaba olvidado	tođo estáƀa ǫlƀiđáđo
me ha dicho eso mismo	me á đíĉo éso mízmo
está en casa	está eŋ kása
de allá era mi amigo	de ąĺá era mj amíɡo
empezó a saltar	empeθo á saltar

82. When a strong vowel is followed by a weak vowel both are pronounced together in a single syllable and the result is phonetically a dipʰthong.

EXAMPLES

firme y sereno	fírme̜i̜ seréno
vaya un enredo	báya u̜n enr̃é̜đo
no hizo nada	nó̜ i̜θo náđa
será imposible	será i̜mposíble

83. When a weak vowel is followed by any vowel, whether strong or weak, both are pronounced together in a single syllable and the weak vowel (first vowel) becomes consonantal. The vowel *i* becomes **j** and the vowel *u* becomes **w**:

EXAMPLES

si es así	sj és así	sjé-sa-sí
ví a Juan	bj á xwán	bjá-xwán
su amigo	sw amígo	swa-mí-go
si a tu amo no	sj a tw ámo nó	sja-twá-mo-nó
su historia	sw istórja	swis-to-rja

NOTE. — It should be remembered that in all the above cases synalepha is the rule in familiar Spanish conversation and in poetry, but not absolutely required. In slow, ceremonious speech and in other cases, as already stated in § **79**, hiatus between the vowels in question may take place.

SYNERESIS

84. When vowels belonging ordinarily to different syllables come together within a word (instead of between words) and they are pronounced together in one syllable the phenomenon is called syneresis. Syneresis in Spanish is as common as synalepha and in general is subject to the same rules. The following observations, however, are important.

1. When the word in question is the emphatic word of a phonic group or is at the end of a phonic group hiatus is the rule and syneresis is very rare.

2. Like vowels within a word do not contract as frequently as between words, and in such words as leer, creer, paseé, etc., it is common only in rapid and familiar conversation.

3. In some words, such as creencia, mohoso, loor, usage favors hiatus rather than syneresis.

4. In the groups *eo*, *ea*, syneresis is the rule when the accent falls on the last vowel or when the group precedes the accented syllable.

Examples

Hiatus	Syneresis
No se puede creer	No puedo creer todo eso
nó se pwéđe kreęr	nó pwéđo kręr tóđo éso
Eso es lo que desean	No desean irse en seguida
éso es lo ke đeséan	nó đeseán irse en segíđa
Vea para que lo crea	Voy a leer el libro ahora
béa para ke lo kréa	bóy a lęr ęl líbro aǫra

SYNERESIS

No deseamos hacerlo	nó đeseámos aθéɾlo
Voy a telefonearle	bóy a telefoneárle
Ahí va el otro	ái ƀá el ótro
No había nada que hacer	no áƀjá náđa ke aθéɾ
Se paseó todo el día	se paseó tóđo ęl día
Deseaba pelear con él	deseáƀa peleár kon ęl
Teodora y Leonor le vieron	teođórai leonóɾ le ƀjérọn

NOTE. — Rule 4 does not apply absolutely, but in general all such common verbs as desear, pasear, menear, telefonear, etc., are pronounced with syneresis in the groups *eá*, *eó*. In the conjugation of these verbs, therefore, the disyllabic groups *e-a*, *e-o* and the syllabic group *ea*, *eo* may alternate, even in the same tense:

deseo	**de-sé-o**	deseamos	**de-seá-mọs**
deseas	**de-sé-as**	deseáis	**de-seáis**
desea	**de-sé-a**	desean	**de-sé-an**
deseé	**de-se-é**	deseamos	**de-seá-mọs**
deseaste	**de-seás-te**	deseasteis	**de-seás-teis**
deseó	**de-seó**	desearon	**de-seá-rọn**

CHAPTER V

INTONATION

85. Intonation is the musical element in speech-sounds. By intonation we mean, therefore, the variations of pitch (or tone) in language. Every language has its special, characteristic intonation. In Spanish, intonation is of the greatest importance and determines to a great extent the rhythmic harmony of speech-sounds. The study of intonation in Spanish is very difficult and complicated. In learning to speak Spanish, however, English-speaking students should take into account at least the following fundamental observations:

1. At the beginning of a phonic group the voice begins and continues in a relatively low pitch as long as the first accented syllable is not reached.

2. When the first accented syllable of a phonic group is reached the voice rises to a medium high pitch, and this is continued in the following syllables as long as the final accented syllable is not reached.

3. When the last accented syllable of the group is reached the voice falls or rises according to circumstances.

a. The voice falls to a pitch lower even than that of the initial unaccented syllable or syllables in the case of the end of a simple declarative sentence.

b. The voice rises to a higher pitch in the case of an interrogative sentence, or an incomplete sentence interrupted by a pause.

Examples

Declarative sentences :

Low Pitch	Medium High Pitch	Lowest Pitch
Visita-	remos el mu-	seo.
Se mar-	charon a la	calle.
Repasa-	remos la lec-	ción.
Se	fueron al con-	cierto.
Le	gusta la lec-	tura.

Interrogative sentences :

Low Pitch	Medium High Pitch	Highest Pitch
¿ Visita-	remos el mu-	seo ?
¿ Se mar-	charon a la	calle ?
¿ Se	fueron al con-	cierto ?
¿ Le	gusta la lec-	tura ?

CHAPTER VI

AMERICAN-SPANISH PRONUNCIATION

86. There is no such thing as a standard American-Spanish pronunciation. The Spanish of America is fundamentally Castilian and is essentially the same as that of Spain. The correct standard Spanish pronunciation as described in this book, although based on the best and most correct Spanish as spoken today by the educated Spaniards of Old and New Castile, is in general the pronunciation of the Spanish spoken by all educated Spanish-Americans. The following fundamental differences, however, should be carefully noted:

1. In American-Spanish (and also in Andalucía) *c* (before *e* or *i*) and *z* are not pronounced as interdental θ, § **55**, but as a simple dental s, not unlike English *s*.

2. In American-Spanish, Spanish palatal *ll*, ḷ, § **67**, is generally pronounced as a *y* sound, continuant y, § **63**, or semiexplosive ŷ, § **64**. This pronunciation of ll is also widespread in Andalucía and some parts of New Castile.

3. In American-Spanish (and also in Andalucía) *s* is pronounced as a dental s, similar to English *s*, while in standard Spanish it is an alveolar, § **57**.

The three sounds above described as characteristic of American-Spanish are also found in parts of Spain, as already indicated, and are nowhere considered as dialectical or vulgar, not even in Castile. The American and Andalusian pronunciation of these consonants is well known in Castile and hardly noticed when heard.

There are other differences between the Spanish pronunciation of Castile and that of Spanish America, although of minor importance. Slight differences are to be found also in the pronunciation of the various countries of Spanish America and in the various provinces of Spain. But everywhere in the Spanish-speaking world the correct standard Spanish pronunciation of Castile as described in this book is considered the best, and students of Spanish should learn only this correct standard Spanish.

CHAPTER VII

EXERCISES FOR REVIEW

87. Review: syllabication, §§ **9–10**; linking of final consonants, §§ **76–78**; synalepha, §§ **79–83**; syneresis, § **84**; intonation, § **85**. Read the following sentences by syllables, pronouncing all the sounds slowly and carefully.

Nosotros aprendemos.

no-só-tro-sa-pren-dé-mọs

Aprendemos el español.

a-pren-dé-mo-se-les-pa-ŋól

Deseamos viajar por España.

de-seá-mọz-ƀja-xár-po-res-pá-ŋa

Vivo en los Estados Unidos.

ƀí-ƀoen-lo-ses-tá-đo-su-ní-đọs

Vino a visitar a su hermano.

ƀí-noa-ƀi-si-tá-ra-swẹr-má-no

Si eso es lo que hicieron.

sjé-soéz-lo-kẹ̦-θjé-rọn

Digo eso porque es la verdad.

dí-goé-so-pọr-kéz-la-ƀẹr-đáđ

Desea saber como están.	de-sé-a-sa-ƀę́r-ko-mo͡es-tán
Y era así como él decía.	yé-ra-sí-ko-mo͡él-de-θí-a
Sus hijos estaban en España.	su-sí-xo-ses-tá-ƀa-ne-nes-pá-ṇa
No me quiere a mi sino a él.	no-me-kjé-re͡a-mí-si-no͡a-ę́l
Va a hablarle a usted.	bá a-ƀlár-le͡au̦s-tę́đ [1]

88. Review the front vowels, §§ 24–28. Read slowly and carefully, distinguishing between the closed and open vowels, if possible even in the case of closed and open *i*, which are represented by the same phonetic symbol.

Este libro es mío y ése es tuyo.	éste líƀro͡ ez mío yése és túyo
Siempre insiste en venir.	sjémprę ịnsíste͡ em be-nír
¿ Qué quieres decir con eso?	ké kjérez đeθír kon éso
Tienen seis peines muy bonitos	tjénen sę́įs pę́įnez mwí ƀonítọs

---

[1] For the sake of uniformity the *d* of **usted** is represented as *đ* in all exercises. As a matter of fact, however, it is usually silent in familiar conversation. See § **74**, (**5**).

Escriben los ejercicios bien.

eskríben los ęxęrθíθjǫz ƀjén

¿ En qué país viven ellos?

eŋ ké paíz ƀíƀen élǫs

Aquí viven los ingleses.

akí ƀíƀen los iŋgléses

No le dejes entrar allí.

nó le đéxes entrár ałí

Ese reloj no anda bien.

ésę ŗęló no ánda ƀjén

Vino y se fué sin decir nada.

bínǫį̦ se fwé sin deθír náđa

¿ Puede usted distinguirlos?

pwéđę ųstéđ đistiŋgírlǫs

Las lecciones son difíciles.

laz lęgθjónes sǫn difíθiles

Quiero saber si es verdad.

kjéro saƀęr sj éz ƀęrđáđ

Es mejor repetir el ejercicio.

éz męxǫr ŗępetír el ęxęrθíθjo

La tierra está bien cultivada.

la tjęŗa está ƀjéŋ kultiƀáđa

El rey respondió entonces.

ęl ŗéį̦ ŗespǫndjó entǫnθes

Yo no me quejo por eso.

yó nó me kęxo por éso

Vas a perder el papel.

bás a pęrđér ęl papęl

89. Review: the vowel a, §§ **29–30**; the back vowels, §§ **31–35**. Read slowly and carefully, distinguishing between the closed and open vowels, if possible even in the case of closed and open *u*, which are represented by the same phonetic symbol.

Vivimos en los Estados Unidos.	biƀímos en los estáđos uníđọs
Nosotros estudiamos demasiado.	nosótros estuđjámọz đemasjáđo
Ahora cuentan los números.	aọra kwéntan lọz númerọs
Voy a mi clase de español.	bó ya mi kláse đe es-pañọl
El niño echó a correr.	ẹl níŋo eĉo á kọrrẹ́r
¿ Por dónde entramos nosotros?	pọr đọ́nde entrámọz nosótrọs
Compró unas rosas para su madre.	kọmpró ụnaz r̄ọsas para su máđre
Compraron alfombras y cuadros.	kọmpráron alfọ́mbras i kwáđrọs
Su madre le cuida muy bien.	su máđre le kwíđa mwí ƀjén
Busca una pluma que perdió.	búska ụna plúma ke pẹrđjó
La luz entra por la ventana.	la lúθ éntra pọr la ƀentána
Son asuntos importantes.	són asúntos impọrtántes
Cuando venga se lo dirás.	kwando ƀénga se lo đirás

Le rogó que fuera a verlo.

lę r̥ǫgó ke fwéra a ƀęrlo

Se ha llevado un disgusto.

se á ļeƀáđo ųn dizgústo

Nuestro instructor es justo.

nwestrǫ i̭nstruktor és xústo

Tú has sido la causa de todo.

tw ás síđo la káųsa đe tóđo

Aprendo porque estudio mucho.

apréndo pǫrke estúđjo múĉo

Su hermano llegó corriendo.

sw ęrmáno ļegó kǫr̃jéndo

Eso costó sólo un duro.

éso kǫstó sólo ųn dúro

Buenos días, señor.

bwénǫz días sęn̥ǫ́r

¿ Cómo está usted hoy?

kómo está ųstéđ ói̭

Oigo algo pero no entiendo.

ói̭go álgo pero no éntjéndo

90. Review the diphthongs, § **36.** In the following sentences observe that some of the diphthongs are between words.

Aquí no hay aire fresco.

akí no ái̭ ái̭re frésko [1]

Yo no soy la causa de su enfado.

yó nó sói̭ la káųsa đe sw ęm̥fáđo

[1] Also: akí noá yâi̭re frésko.

Hoy voy a bailar mucho.	ói ƀó ya ƀai̯lár múĉo
Esa ley no me gusta a mí.	ésa léi̯ nó me gústa͡ a mí
Iba y venía de prisa.	íƀai̯ ƀenía đe prísa
Hoy trabajé seis horas.	ói̯ traƀaxé séi̯s óras
Compró un automóvil.	ko̜mpró u̜n au̜tomóƀil
Entré y se lo dije.	entré̜i̯ se lo đíxe
Estaba a una legua de camino	estáƀa a͡ u̜na légwa đe kamíno
Hay que pagar las deudas.	ái̯ ke pagár laz đéu̜đas

91. Review: the bilabial and labiodental consonants, §§ 44–49; the linking of final *y*, § 77.

Ponga usted los papeles aquí.	pó̜ŋga͡ u̜stę́đ lo̜s papéles akí
Vámonos pronto por ellos.	bámono̜s pró̜nto por é̜lo̜s
Aquí vivo en el invierno.	akí ƀíƀo͡ en el imbję́rno
Tal vez le tengan envidia.	tal ƀę́ż le té̜ŋgan embíđja
El pobre estaba enfermo.	e̜l pó̜bre͡ estáƀa͡ em̜fę́rmo
Aquí vivía el infeliz.	akí ƀiƀía el im̜felíθ

No quieren venir ahora.	no kjérem benír aǫra
Me obligaron a venir.	me obligáron a benír
Vinieron bien vestidos.	binjérǫm bjém bestíđǫs
Han venido muy cansados.	ám beníđo mwí kansáđǫs
Quiere un vaso de agua.	kjére um báso đe ágwa
Soy un verdadero amigo.	só yúm bęrđađéro amígo
Ya no podemos vivir.	yá nó pođémǫz bibír
He venido en vez de él.	é beníđo em bę́z đe ę́l
Voy a ser muy breve.	bó ya sęr mwí brébe
Son verdaderos amigos.	sǫ́m bęrđađéros amígǫs
Hablamos español bien.	ablámos espaŋǫ́l bjén

92. Review the dental and interdental consonants, §§ 50–56.

Tú tienes tiempo para todo.	tú tjénes tjémpo para tóđo
No tengo tiempo para nada.	nó téŋgo tjémpo para náđa

Toma este libro y da-me ése.

tóma éste líbroi ɖá-me ése

Dame el dinero pronto.

dáme ęl dinéro prǫnto

Desea vender la tienda.

deséa ƀendę̨r la tjénda

¿ Qué andan diciendo de mí?

ke ándan diθjéndo ɖe mí

Cuando venga se lo dices.

kwando ƀeŋga se lo ɖíθes

Esa debe ser su edad.

ésa ɖéƀe sę̨r sw eɖáɖ

Yo le dí más dinero.

yó le ɖí máz ɖinéro

Los dos debemos dar algo.

lǫz ɖǫ́z ɖeƀémǫz ɖár álgo

Han estado bastante o-cupados.

án estáɖo ƀastánte o-kupáɖǫs

Ella siempre dice la verdad.

éļa sjémpre ɖíθe la ƀę̨rɖáɖ

Lleva manzanas en la cesta.

ļéƀa manθánas en la θésta

El padre de Eduardo es débil.

ęl páɖre ɖe eɖwárɖo éz ɖéƀil

No debemos hacer eso.

nó ɖeƀémos aθér éso

Desde entonces no he dado nada.

dézɖe entǫ́nθes no é ɖáɖo náɖa

Ha ido a los Estados Unidos.

a íɖo a los estáɖos uníɖǫs

Yo voy allí todos los años.

yó ƀó yaļí tóɖǫz los ánǫs

93. Review: the alveolar consonants, §§ 57–62;
the various sounds of **n**, §§ **47, 49, 59, 73.**

Ésa es la suya y ésta
la mía.

ésa éz la súya yésta
la mía

Siempre salen con la
suya.

sjémpre sáleŋ kọn la
súya

Lo que dice no es ver-
dad.

lo ke đíθe no éz b̦ẹr-
đáđ

Éste es mío y aquél
es de él.

éste éz mío yakel
éz đe ẹ́l

Tengo que comprar
unas botas.

téŋgo ke kọmprár
únaz b̦ótas

Yo no les tengo en-
vidia.

yó nó les téŋgo em-
bíđja

Vale solamente dos
reales.

b̦ále solaménte đọ̆z
r̄eáles

¿Con qué pagas los
billetes?

kọŋ ké págaz lọz
b̦iḷétes

El enfermo está en
peligro.

el eɱfẹ́rmo está em
pelígro

Siempre come sin ga-
nas.

sjémpre kóme siŋ gá-
nas

La casa está enfrente
de aquí.

la kása está eɱfrénte
đe akí

Déjelos usted en paz.

đẹ́xelos ustéđ em páθ

Olvidé los papeles.

ọlb̦iđé lọs papéles

He recibido dos mil reales.

ę r̄éθibíđo đǫz míl r̄eáles

Todos estaban alrededor de él.

tóđos estában alr̄ę̆đeđǫ́r đe ę́l

Esta tierra es muy rica.

ésta tję́r̄a éz mwí r̄íka

Éste sí que es un enredo.

éste sí ke és ún en-r̄ę́đo

Es muy caro el carro.

éz mwí káro ęl kár̄ǫ

Rojo se escribe con jota.

r̄ǫ́xo se eskríbe kǫŋ xóta

Barril se escribe con erre.

bar̄íl se eskríbe kon ę́r̄ę̆

Ahora se ahorra usted eso.

aǫ́ra   se aǫ́r̄a ᶙstéđ éso

94. Review the palatal and velar consonants, §§ 63–73.

Ayer vino a llamarme.

ayę́r ƀíno a ḷamárme

¿ Están ya en la calle?

están ŷá en la káḷe

Llévese usted el hielo.

ḷéƀesę̆ ᶙstéđ ęl ŷélo

¿ Está ya bien preparado?

está yá ƀjém pre-paráđo

Los muchachos juegan mucho.

lǫz muĉáĉǫs xwégan muĉo

Mañana son los exámenes.

mañána   sǫ́n los ęgsámenes

Yo les tengo mucho cariño.	yó les téŋgo múĉo karíṇo
Llegaron el año pasado.	legáron el áṇo pasáđo
Ellos dicen que callarán.	élọz đíθeŋ ke kaḷarán
Ella no ha llegado todavía.	éḷa no á ḷegáđo tođabía
Dejó olvidada la capa.	dẹxọ́ ọlƀiđáđa la kápa
La gente quiere explicaciones.	la xénte kjére esplikaθjónes
¿ Quién le dijo lo del juego?	kjén le đíxo lo đẹl xwégo
Tengo ganas de comer helado.	téŋgo gánaz đe komér eláđo
Creo que lo han engañado.	kréo ke lo án eŋgaṇáđo
Yo hago lo que me da la gana.	yo ágo lo ke me đá la gána
Alguna cosa tenemos que decir.	algúna kósa tenémọs ke đeθír
Ha tenido un gran éxito.	á teníđo ụŋ grán ẹ́gsito
Mataron un gallo ayer.	matáron uŋ gáḷo ayẹ́r
No supo bien la lección.	nó súpo ƀjén la lẹgθjọ́n
Es un general distinguido.	és úŋ xenerál distiŋgíđo

95. Review: silent consonants, § 74; liaison or linking, §§ 76–77; pronunciation of the conjunction y, § 78; synalepha, §§ 79–83; syneresis, § 84.

El cuarto estaba muy oscuro.

el kwárto estába mwí ǫskúro

No me gusta ese reloj.

no me gústa ése r̦ęló

Deseamos estudiar psicología.

deseámos estuɟjár sikolǫxía

Voy a telefonear en seguida.

bó ya telefoneár en segíɖa

Le hemos dicho que se subscriba.

le émǫz ɖiĉo ke se suskríba

En septiembre iré allá.

en setjémbrę i̦ré al̦á

Voy a ver si es verdad.

bó ya b̦ęr sj éz b̦ęrɖáɖ

Por eso no ha venido.

por éso no á beníɖo

La alcoba es muy hermosa.

la alkóba éz mwi ęrmósa

Así soy yo, señor.

así sǫ̦i yó seņǫ̦r

No puedo acompañarlos.

nó pwéɖo akǫmpaņárlǫs

Yo me llamo Antonio.

yó me l̦ámo antónjo

Hay algo sobre la mesa.

á yálgo sóbre la mésa

No era necesario hacerlo.

no éra neθesárjo aθȩ́rlo

Empezó a llorar y a gritar.

empeθo á ḷorár ya gritár

Fernando es más alto que Eduardo.

fẹrnándo éz más álto ke eđwárđo

Su hermano es médico.

sw ẹrmáno éz méđiko

Ya estaba casi obscuro.

yá estába kasj ǫskúro

Mi alcoba es pequeña.

mj alkóba és pekéṇa

Si es como dice, váyase.

sj és komo đíθe báyase

No olvidaré sus fa-vores.

nǫ ǫlbiđaré sus fa-bóres

Vendo manzanas y naranjas.

béndo manθánas i naráŋxas

Y él no dijo ni una palabra.

yẹl nó đíxo nj úna palábra

Tú eres el peor de todos.

tw éres ẹl peór đe tóđǫs

Yo no creo que sea verdad.

yó nó kréo ke séa bẹrđáđ

Mi amigo estaba ahí también.

mj amígo estába ái tambjén

El triunfo fué gran-de y solemne

el trjúɱfo fwé grán-dẹị solemne

NOTE.—The student must keep in mind that in all the words and sentences given as examples the phonetic transcription represents the typical standard Spanish pronunciation. In many cases, however, slight variations are possible within the rules given and according to the various conditions of rapidity, slowness, familiarity, and formality of speech articulation. In the sentence *Yo no creo que sea verdad*, for example, the words *creo* and *sea* may be monosyllabic in familiar and rapid speech. Such cases of syneresis are common in familiar conversation and in poetry. Synalepha, of course, is often subject to the same conditions.

CHAPTER VIII

PHONETIC TEXTS

96. In the following phonetic texts *the most correct standard Spanish pronunciation is given in all cases and variant pronunciations even when considered correct are not given.* Syllabic division is indicated only in the first two texts. In the remaining texts syllabic division is not indicated and the student should observe carefully the question of closed and open syllables, final consonants that form syllables with the initial vowels of words that follow, etc. See §§ 76–78. Synalepha and syneresis are represented by the sign used in previous exercises, me ha dicho **me͡ á điĉo**, deseamos ir **dese͡ámos ír,** and the vowels thus united should be always pronounced in one syllable. See §§ 79–83. In the case of like vowels synalepha means, of course, contraction into one vowel, se está **se͡ está,** § 80. Phonic or breath groups are represented in the following manner: A double line ‖ represents a final pause, ordinarily a pause indicated orthographically by a period (sometimes also a colon or semicolon), a pause lasting about one second. A single line ǀ represents a pause

of about half a second, and a half line ǀ indicates
the briefest pause, one lasting about a quarter of a
second.

97.

Los días de la semana

En una semana hay
siete días. Los días de
la semana son el domin-
go, el lunes, el martes, el
miércoles, el jueves, el
viernes y el sábado. El
lunes, el martes, el miércoles, el jueves, el viernes y el sábado son
días de trabajo. Los
lunes, los martes, los
miércoles, los jueves y
los viernes vamos a la escuela. El domingo es
día de descanso. Ese
día vamos a la iglesia.
Yo voy a la iglesia todos
los domingos.

El domingo es el pri-
mer día de la semana.
Es el primero. El lunes
es el segundo día de la

lǫz-đí-az-đe-la-se-má-na
e-nú-na-se-má-náį̂-
sjé-te-đí-as‖ lǫz-đí-az-đe-
la-se-má-na-só-nęl do-míŋ-
goǀ ęl-lú-nesǀ ęl-már-tesǀ ęl
mjęr-ko-lesǀ ęl xwé-ƀes ęl-
ƀjęr-nez-yęl-sá-ƀa-đo‖ ęl-
lú-nesǀ ęl-már-tesǀ ęl-mjęr-
ko-lesǀ ęl xwé-ƀesǀ ęl ƀjęr-
nez-yęl-sá-ƀa-đoǀ sǫn-
dí-az-đe-tra-ƀá-xo‖ lǫz-
lú-nesǀ lǫz-már-tesǀ lǫz-
mjęr-ko-lesǀ lǫs-xwé-ƀe-si-
lǫz-ƀjęr-nesǀbá-mo-sa-laes-
kwé-la‖ ęl-do-míŋ-goéz-
đí-a-đe-đes-kán-so‖ é-se-
đí-a-ƀá-mo-sa-laį̂-glé-sja‖
yó-vó-ya-laį̂-glé-sja-tó-đǫz-
lǫz-đo-míŋ-gǫs‖

ęl-do-míŋ-goé-sęl-pri-
męr-đí-a-đe-la-se-má-na‖
é-sęl-pri-mé-ro‖ ęl-lú-ne-
sé-sęl-se-gún-do-đí-a-đe-la-

semana y el martes es el tercero. El sábado es el último día de la semana. Yo no voy a la escuela los sábados. Los sábados por la mañana trabajo en mi casa. Por las tardes estudio o salgo a pasearme.

se-má-na⎸ yẹl-már-te-sé-sẹl-tẹr-θé-ro‖ẹl-sá-ƀa-đoé-se-lúl-ti-mo-đí-a-đe- la-se-má-na‖ yó-nó-vó-ya-laes-kwé-la-lọs-sá-ƀa-đọs‖ lọs-sá-ƀa-đọs-pọr-la - ma - ṇá - na - tra - ƀá-xoen-mi-ká-sa‖ pọr las-tár - đe - ses -tú-đjo-o-sál-goa-pa-seár-me‖

98.
El estudio del español

En los Estados Unidos el estudio del español es de muy grande importancia. Las dos lenguas importantes de América son el inglés y el español. El inglés es la lengua oficial de casi toda la América del Norte y el español es la lengua oficial de casi toda la Améri-

e - les - tú - đjo - đe-les-pa-ṇọ́l

en - lo-ses-tá-đo-su-ní-đọs⎸ - e-les-tú-đjo-đe-les-pa-ṇó- léz-đe-mwí-grán-dẹịm-pọr-tán-θja‖ laz-đọ́z - léŋ - gwa - sim-por-tán-tez-đea-mé-ri-ka⎸ só-ne - liŋ - gléz - ye - les-pa-ṇọ́l‖ e-liŋ-glé-séz-la-léŋ - gwao - fi - θjál-de-ká-si - tó - đa - la - mé - ri - ka-đẹl-nọ́r-te⎸ ye-les-pa-ṇó-lés - la - leŋ - gwao - fi-θjál-de - ká - si - tó - đa-la-mé-rica del Sur. Las relaciones diplomáticas, intelectuales y comerciales entre las dos Américas hacen muy necesario el estudio del español en las escuelas de los Estados Unidos. Si hemos de conocer bien a los españoles y a los hispano-americanos y comprender su civilización, tenemos que estudiar su historia, su vida nacional y su modo de pensar. Para estudiar la historia, la vida y la cultura de los países españoles es de capital importancia tener un buen conocimiento de la lengua española. Para llegar a conocer a la España grande, la Espa-

ka-đęl-súr‖ laz r̦ę-la-
θjó-nez-đi-plo-má-ti-kas|
in-te-lęk-twá-le-si-ko-
męr-θjá-le-sen-tre-laz-
đó-sa-mé-ri-kas| á-θen-
mwí-ne-θe-sá-rjoe-les-
tú-đjo-đe-les-pa-ŋó-len-
la-ses-kwé-laz-đe-lo-
ses-tá-đo-su-ní-đǫs‖ sjé-
mǫz-đe-ko-no-θęr-bjé-
na-lo-ses-pa-ŋó-lez-ya-
lo-sis-pá-noa-me-ri-ká-
nǫs| i-kǫm-pren-dęr-su-
θi-bi-li-θa-θjǫ́n| te-né-
mǫs-kes-tu-đjár-swis-
tó-rja| su-bí-đa-na-θjo-
nál| i-su-mó-đo-đe-pen-
sár‖ pa-raes-tu-đjár-
laįs-tó-rja| la-bí-đaį-la-
kul-tú-ra-đe-lǫs-pa-í-se-
ses-pa-ŋó-les| éz| đe-ka-
pi-tá-lim-pǫr-tán-θja-te-
né-rúm-bwéŋ-ko-nó-θi-
mjén-to-đe-la-léŋ-
gwaes-pa-ŋóla‖ pa-ra-lę-
gá-ra-ko-no-cé-ra-laes-
pá-ŋa-grán-de| laes-pá-

ña espiritual, tenemos que estudiar a los que escriben su lengua y representan su cultura.

ṇaes-pi-ri-twál| te-né-moṣ-kes-tu-đjá-ra-loṣ-kes-krí-ƀen-su-léŋ-gwai̯-r̨ę-pre-sén-tan-su-kul-tú-ra‖

99.

Refranes

Vale más saber que tener.

La pereza es llave de la pobreza.

De la mano a la boca se pierde la sopa.

Cada oveja con su pareja.

Haz bien y no mires a quien.

Quien mucho abarca poco aprieta.

El que adelante no mira atrás se queda.

r̨ęfránes

bále más saƀ̨ęr[1] ke ten̨ęr‖

la peréθa̧ éz ḽáƀe đe la poƀréθa‖

de la máno a la ƀóka̧ se pj̨ęrđe la sópa‖

káđa oƀ̨ęxa̧ koṇ su par̨ęxa‖

áẓ ƀj̨éņ i no míres a kj̨én‖

kj̨en múĉo aƀárka̧ póko aprj̨éta‖

ęl ke ađelánte nó míra̧ atrás se kéđa‖

100.

Cantares

En enero no hay claveles porque los marchita el hielo ;

kantáres

en enéro no ái̯ klaƀéles porke loẓ marĉíta el ŷélo‖

en tu cara los hay siempre
porque lo permite el cielo.

Tus ojos copian el día :
los entornas, amanece ;
los abres, el sol deslum-
　　bra ;
los cierras, la noche viene.

Aunque　　tengas　　más
　　amores
que flores tiene un almen-
　　dro,
ninguno te ha de querer
como yo te estoy que-
　　riendo.

101.

Caperucita Encarnada

Una vez había en un
pueblo una niña lo más
linda que verse puede.
Su madre estaba loca
con ella, y su abuela más
loca todavía.　La abuela
le mandó hacer una cape-
rucita encarnada, la cual
le sentaba tan bien que en

en tu kára los ái sjémpre⌐
pǫrke lo pęrmíte ęl θjélo‖

tus ǫxǫs kópjan ęl día|
los entǫ́rnas| amanéθe|
los áþres| ęl sǫ́l dezlúm-
　　bra|
lǫs θjḗras| la nóĉe þjéne‖

aųŋke téŋgaz más amó-
　　res⌐
ke flóres tjéne ųn alménd-
　　dro⌐
niŋgúno te á đe kerę́r
komo yó te estǫ́i ke-
　　rjéndo‖

kaperuθíta eŋkarnáđa

úna þéθ aþía en úm
pwéblo ųna níṇa| lo máz
línda ke þę́rse pwéđe‖
su máđre estáþa　lóka
kon éḷa| i sw aþwéla máz
lóka tođaþía‖　la aþwéla
le mando áθér una kape-
ruθíta eŋkarnáđa| la kwál
le sentáþa tam bjén|ke en

todas partes la llama-
ban Caperucita En-
carnada.

Un día su madre co-
ció al horno unas tortas, y
le dijo :

— Vé a ver cómo está
tu abuela, porque me han
dicho que está en-
ferma. Llévale esta tor-
ta y esta orcita de man-
teca.

Caperucita Encarnada
se marchó inmediata-
mente para ir a casa de
su abuela, que vivía en
otro pueblo. Al pasar
por un bosque se en-
contró con el lobo a
quien le dieron ganas de
comérsela. Pero no se a-
trevió porque unos leña-
dores estaban cerca. El
lobo le preguntó a la
niña adónde iba, y la
niña le respondió :

tóðas pártez la ḷamá-
ƀaŋ   kaperuθíta eŋ-
karnáða‖

ún día su máðre ko-
θjo ál ǫrnó unas tǫrtas∣ i
le ðíxo∣

be á ƀę́r kómo está
tw aƀwéla∣ pǫrke me án
díĉo   ke está eɱ-
férma‖ ḷéƀale ésta tǫr-
ta∣ yésta ǫrθíta ðe man-
téka‖

kaperuθíta eŋkarnáða
se   marĉǫ́ ịnmeðjáta-
ménte∣ pará ịr a kása ðe
sw aƀwéla∣ ke ƀiƀía en
ótro pwéƀlo‖ al pasár
por úm bǫ́ske se eŋ-
kǫntró kon ęl lóƀo∣ a
kjen le ðjérǫŋ gánaz ðe
komę́rsela‖ pero nó se a-
treƀjó pǫrké ųnǫz leɲa-
ðóres estáƀan θę́rka‖ ęl
lóƀo le pregunto á la
níɲa aðónde íƀa∣ i la
níɲa lę r̃espǫndjó‖

— Voy a ver a mi a-
buela y a llevarle una
torta y una orcita de
manteca que mi madre
le envía.

— ¿ Vive muy lejos
de aquí? — dijo el lobo.

— ¡ Oh ! sí — con-
testó Caperucita Encar-
nada, — pasado el molino
que ves allá abajo, en la
primera casa del pueblo.

— Bueno — dijo el lo-
bo ; — yo también quie-
ro ir a verla. Yo iré por
este camino y tú por
ese otro, y ya veremos
quien llega primero.

El lobo echó a correr
con todas sus fuerzas
por aquel camino, que e-
ra el más corto, y la
niña se marchó por el
más largo, entretenién-
dose en coger avellanas,

bóya ƀér a mja-
ƀwéla‖ ya ḷeƀárle u̯na
tǫ́rta yúna ǫrθíta đe
mantéka ke mi máđre
le embía‖

bíƀe mwí lę́xǫz
đe akí‖ díxo ęl lóƀo‖

ó sí‖ kǫn-
testó kaperuθíta eŋkar-
náđa‖ pasáđo el molíno
ke ƀés aḷá aƀáxo en la
priméra kása đęl pwéƀlo‖

bwéno‖ díxo ęl ló-
ƀo‖ ŷó tambjén kjé-
rǫ i̯r a ƀę́rla‖ ŷǫ́ i̯ré por
éste kamínǫ i̯ tú por
ése ótro‖ i yá ƀerémǫs
kjén ḷéga priméro‖

ęl lóƀo eƀo á kǫr̃ę́r
kǫn tóđas sus fwę́rθas
por akę́l kamíno‖ ke é-
ra ęl más kǫ́rto‖ i la
nína se marƀó por ęl
máz lárgo‖ entretenjén-
dose eŋ kǫxér aƀeḷánas‖

en perseguir mariposas
y en hacer ramilletes de
las florecillas que en-
contraba al paso.

No tardó mucho el
lobo en llegar a casa de
la abuela. Luego que
llegó, llamó : tan, tan.
— ¿ Quién es?
— Es tu nieta, Ca-
perucita Encarnada —
contestó el lobo, imitando
la voz de la niña, — que
te trae una torta y una orcita de manteca de
parte de su madre.

La abuela, que estaba
enferma en la cama,
gritó :
— Levanta el pica-
porte.

El lobo levantó el
picaporte y la puerta se
abrió. Entonces se arro-
jó sobre la pobre mujer
y la devoró en un abrir

---

em pɛrsegír maripósas
yen aθɛ́r ꞧamiḷétez đe
las floreθíḷas ke eŋ‿
kontrába al páso‖

nó tarđô mûĉo el
lóƀo en ḷegár a kása đe
la aƀwéla‖ lwégo ke
ḷegó˞ ḷamó| tán| tán‖
kjén és‖
és tu njéta˞ ka-
peruθíta eŋkarnáđa|
kǫntesto ɛl lóƀo˞ imitándo
la ƀǫ́z đe la níɲa| ke
te tráe úna tǫ́rta yúna ǫr‿
θíta đe mantéka˞ de
párte đe su máđre‖
la aƀwéla ke está-
ƀa emfɛ́rma en la káma˞
gritó|
leƀánta ɛl pika-
pǫ́rte‖
ɛl lóƀo leƀantó ɛl
pikapǫ́rte˞ i la pwɛ́rta
se aƀrjó‖ entǫ́nθes se aꞧǫ-
xó soƀre la póƀre muxɛ́r˞
i la đeƀoro én ún aƀrír

y cerrar de ojos. Luego cerró la puerta y fué a acostarse en la cama de la abuela para esperar a Caperucita Encarnada.

Caperucita Encarnada llegó y llamó: tan, tan.

— ¿ Quién es?

Caperucita Encarnada se asustó al oír la voz del lobo; pero creyendo que su abuela estaba acatarrada, respondió:

Es tu nieta, Caperucita Encarnada, que te trae una torta y una orcita de manteca de parte de su madre.

El lobo, dulcificando un poco su voz, le gritó:

— Levanta el picaporte.

Caperucita Encarnada levantó el picaporte y la puerta se abrió.

i θeɾár ðe ọxọs‖ lwégo θẹɾọ́ la pwẹ́rta| i fwe ákọstárse en la káma ðe la aðwéla| para esperár a kaperuθíta eŋkarnáða‖

kaperuθíta eŋkarnáða lẹgọ́ i lamọ́| tán| tán‖ kjén és‖

kaperuθíta eŋkarnáða se asusto ál oír la ðọz ðẹl lóðo| pero kreyéndo ke sw aðwéla estáða akataɾáða| ɾespọndjó|

és tu njéta| kaperuθíta eŋkarnáða |ke te tráe úna tọ́rta yúna ọrθíta ðe mantéka ðe párte ðe su mádre‖

ẹl lóðo| dulθifikándo ụm póko su ðọz le gritó|

leðánta ẹl pikapọ́rte‖

kaperuθíta eŋkarnáða leðanto ẹl pikapọ́rte| i la pwẹ́rta se aðrjó‖

La niña entró y el lobo le dijo :

— Pon la torta y la orcita de manteca sobre la mesa y ven a acostarte conmigo.

Caperucita Encarnada fué a meterse en la cama y quedó asombrada al ver cómo estaba formada su abuela.

— Abuela, ¡ qué brazos tan largos tienes !

— ¡ Para abrazarte mejor, hija mía !

— Abuela, ¡ qué piernas tan grandes tienes !

— ¡ Para correr mejor, hija mía !

— Abuela, ¡ qué orejas más grandes tienes !

— ¡ Para oírte mejor, hija mía !

— Abuela, ¡ qué ojos más grandes tienes !

— ¡ Para verte mejor, hija mía !

la níṇa entró‖ yẹl lóƀo le đíxo‖

pǫ́n la tǫ́rta i̥ la ǫrθíta đe mantéka soƀre la mésa‖ i ƀén a akǫstarte kǫnmígo‖‖

kaperuθíta eŋkarnáđa fwe á metẹ́rse en la káma‖ i keđo ásǫmbráđa al ƀẹ́r kómo estáƀa fǫrmáđa sw aƀwéla‖‖

aƀwéla‖ ké ƀráθǫs tan lárgǫs tjénes‖‖

para aƀraθárte mẹxǫ́r‖ íxa mía‖‖

aƀwéla‖ ké pjẹ́rnas taŋ grándes tjénes‖‖

para kǫřẹ́r mẹxǫ́r‖ íxa mía‖‖

aƀwéla‖ ke óřẹ́xaz máz grándes tjénes‖‖

para oírte mẹxǫ́r‖ íxa mía‖‖

aƀwéla‖ ké ǫ́xǫz máz grándes tjénes‖‖

para ƀẹ́rte mẹxǫ́r‖ íxa mía‖‖

— Abuela, ¡ qué dientes más grandes y afilados tienes !

— ¡ Para comerte mejor, hija mía !

Y al decir estas palabras el infame lobo se arrojó sobre la niña y se la comió.

aƀwéla‖ ké đjéntez máz grández yafiládos tjénes‖

para komę́rte mę̆xǫ̆r‖ íxa mía‖

yal deθír éstas palá‿bras‖el im̥fáme lóƀo se a‿r̃ǫxó soƀre la níᶇa‖ i se la komjó‖

102.

El Cantor de la Miseria

En la traza, uno de tantos juglares callejeros, truhanes, desvergonzados, era el poeta avasallador de la multitud, de la multitud miserable, sufridora de todos los dolores, sin sentido del propio sufrimiento.

Desde el amanecer, errante por la ciudad, atravesaba las calles principales, donde la nobleza, el poderío, el trá-

ęl kantǫ̆r đe la misérja‖

en la tráθa‖ úno đe tántǫs xugláres kaļę̆xérǫs‖ truánes‖ dezƀę̆r‿gǫnθáđǫs‖ éra ęl poéta a‿basaļađǫ̆r đe la multitúđ‖ de la multitúđ miseráƀle‖ sufriđóra đe tó‿đǫz lǫz đolóres‖ sin sentí‿đo đęl própjo sufrimjénto‖

dezđe‿el amaneθę̆r‖ ę̆r̃ánte pǫr la θjuđáđ‖ atraƀesába las káļes prinθipáles‖ dǫ́nde la no‿ƀléθa‖ ęl pođerío‖ ęl trá-

fico mostrábanse inso-
lentes, sin pararse a cantar una sola vez, pero al
pasar lento, contem-
plador melancólico del
expansivo bullicio, re-
cogía en el alma indig-
nación y tristeza.

En las calles apartadas
del centro, de tenebrosas
viviendas amontonadas,
respiradores pestilentes
de sus moradores misera-
bles, cantaba el juglar
rodeado de pobre gente,
ignorante, haraposa,
hambrienta; cantaba
con ira santa de poeta algunas veces, otras aba-
tido, desconsolado; Cris-
to humano sin divinidad
de Redentor; otras veces
estrofas sin sentido, pero
resplandecientes de ar-
monía, letanías de amor
que penetraban el alma

fiko| mọstrábansẹ i̥nso-
léntes|sim parárse a kan-
tár úna sóla ƀẹ̆θ| pero al
pasa̠r lénto| kọntem-
plađọ̆r melaŋkóliko đel
espansíƀo ƀu̥líθjo| r̄ẹ-
kọxía en el álma i̥ndig-
naθjón i tristéθa‖

en las kále̠s apartáđaz
đel θéntro| de teneƀrósaz
ƀiƀjéndas amontonáđas|
r̄espirađóres pestiléntez
đe suz morađórez miserá-
ƀles| kantáƀa ẹl xuglár
r̄ọđeáđo đe póƀre xénte|
ignoránte| arapósa|
ambrjénta‖ kantáƀa
kon íra sánta đe poéta al-
gúnaz ƀéθes| ótras aƀa-
tíđo| deskọnsoláđo‖ krís-
to u̥máno sin diƀiniđáđ
đẹ r̄ẹđentór‖ ótraz ƀéθes
estrófas sin sentíđo| perọ
r̄esplandeθjéntez đe ar-
monía| letaníaz đe amọ́r
ke penetráƀan el álma

con su aroma de todos
los amores, y en cuantos
le escuchaban, rodeán-
dole apretados, devora-
dores de las palabras, los
rostros cerrados con du-
ra expresión de triste ignorancia, se esclarecían
como iluminados de súbi-
to por interior aurora, y
para siempre ungidos por
la divina poesía, queda-
ban grabadas en su frente
las   santas   palabras
. . . justicia, piedad, esperanza.

Jamás cantó de otros
amores el poeta " Cantor
de la Miseria," como
le llamaban todos. Da-
ma Miseria era su dama,
y nunca tuvo más fiel
amador.

La hija del Rey era
muy aficionada de la
poesía, y aunque cien

kǫn sw aróma ðe tóðǫz
los amóres| yeŋ kwántǫz
le eskučában| r̄ǫðeán-
dole apretáðǫs| deƀora-
ðórez ðe las palábras| lǫz
r̄ǫ́strǫs θer̄áðǫs kǫn dú-
ra espresjǫ́n de trístę i̯g-
noránθja| se esklareθían
komǫ i̯lumináðǫz ðe súƀi-
to por interjór au̯róra| i
para sjémpre u̯ŋxíðǫs pǫr
la ðiƀína poesía| keðá-
ƀaŋ graƀáðas en su frénte
las   santas   palábras|
xustíθja| pjeðáð| es-
peránθa||

xamás kantó ðe ótros
amóres ęl poéta kantǫ́r
ðe la misérja| komo
le l̦amában tóðǫs|| dá-
ma misérja éra su ðáma|
i núŋka túƀo más fjél
amaðǫ́r||

la íxa ðęl r̄éi̯| éra
mwí afiθjonáða ðe   la
poesía| yáu̯ŋke   θjém

poetas cortesanos hala-
gaban de continuo su
vanidad de hermosa y de
princesa, deseaba escu-
char al poeta callejero
de libre espíritu, al que
satirizaba las costumbres
cortesanas, al que amena-
zaba con ruinas y
muertes a los poderosos,
al que no se humillaba a
la hermosura, ni al
poder, ni a la riqueza,
al enamorado " Cantor
de la Miseria" .

Le oyó por fin y lloró al
oírlo, y estaba tan
hermosa llorando triste-
mente tristezas que nun-
ca había sentido, que el
poeta " Cantor de la Mi-
seria " por vez primera
cantó la hermosura de u-
na mujer. Afirmaba la
princesa que poeta algu-
no la había emocionado

poétas kǫrtesános ala-
gában de kǫntínwo su
baniđáđ đęrmósa į đe
prinθésa| deseába esku-
čár al poéta kalęxéro
đe líbre espíritu| al ke
satiriθába las kǫstúmbres
kǫrtesánas| al ke amena-
θába kǫn r̄wínas i
mwę́rtes a lǫs pođerósǫs|
al ke nó se ųmiļába a
la ęrmosúra| nj al
pođę́r| nj a la r̄ikéθa|
al enamoráđo kantǫ́r
đe la misérja||

le oyó pǫr fín| i ļoro ál
oírlo|| yestába tan
ęrmósa ļorándo tríste-
ménte tristéθas ke nún-
ka abía sentíđo| kę ęl
poéta kantǫ́r đe la mi-
sérja pǫr þę́θ priméra
kantó la ęrmosúra đé ų-
na muxę́r|| afirmába la
prinθésa ke poéta algú-
no   la abía emoθjonáđo

tan dulcemente, y afir-
maba el poeta que nadie
como la hermosa prince-
sa había comprendido sus
canciones.

— ¡ Mal hice en escu-
char a tanto poeta corte-
sano! ¿ Qué podían de-
cirme sino mentiras lison-
jeras? Desde hoy tú se-
rás mi poeta preferido.

— ¡ Mal hice en cantar
mis canciones a los mi-
serables! ¿ No es mejor
conmover piadosa-
mente a los poderosos, que
despertar amenazadores
a los humildes? Desde hoy
sólo cantaré para vos.

Y de este modo quedó el
poeta al servicio de
la hija del rey. Con sus
colores, y bordadas las
armas al pecho, sobre el
corazón, le veían cabal-
gar al servicio de la ca-
rroza regia; los misera-

tan dúlθeménte| yafir-
máḃa ęl poéta ke náđje
komo la ęrmósa prinθé-
sa aḃía kọmprendíđo sus
kanθjónes||

mál íθe en esku-
ĉár a tánto poéta kọrte-
sáno|| ké pođían de-
θírme sino mentíraz lisọŋ-
xéras|| dezđe ọ̣i tú se-
raz mi poéta preferíđo||

mál íθe eŋ kantár
mis kanθjónes a lọz mi-
seráḃles|| no éz mẹxọ́r
kọnmoḃę́r pjađósa-
ménte a los pođerósọs ke
đespẹrtár amenaθađóres
a los umíldes|| dezđe ọ̣i
sólo kantaré para ḃọ́s||

i đéste mójđo keđo ę̣l
poéta al sẹrḃíθjo đe
la íxa đẹl r̄ę́i̧|| kọn sus
kolóres' i ḃọr̄đađaz las
ármas al peĉo꞉ soḃrẹ ęl
koraθọ́n| le ḃeían kaḃal-
gár al sẹrḃíθjo đe la ka-
r̄ọ́θa r̄éxja|| lọz miserá-

bles habían perdido a su poeta para siempre, y desde entonces si algún nuevo juglar venía a decirles: "Oídme, yo soy otro Cantor de la Miseria", pasaban de largo, desconfiados, tristes, incrédulos. . . .

¡Bah! "Cantor de la Miseria", hasta que las princesas quieran oírte.

Jacinto Benavente

bles abíam pęrđíđo a su poéta para sjémpre|i đezđe entǫnθes| sj algún nwébo xuglár benía a đeθírles| oíđme| ŷó sóy ótro kantǫr đe la misérja| pasában de lárgo| deskǫm̦fjáđǫs| tristes| iŋkréđulos||

bá| kantǫr đe la misérja| ásta ke las prinθésas kjéran oírte|| xaθínto benabénte||

103.
Romance del Cid

Cabalga Diego Laínez
al buen rey besar la mano;
consigo se los llevaba
los trescientos hijosdalgo.

Entre ellos iba Rodrigo
el soberbio castellano;
todos cabalgan a mula,
sólo Rodrigo a caballo;
todos visten oro y seda,
Rodrigo va bien armado;

 řǫmánθe đęl θíđ

kabálga đjégo laínę̧θ
al bwén řę́i̧ besár la máno|
kǫnsígo se lǫz ḷebába
lǫs tresθjéntos ixǫzđálgo|

entre éḷos íba řǫđrígo|
ęl sobę́rbjo kasteḷáno|
tóđǫs kabalgan a múla|
sólǫ řǫđrígo a kabáḷo|
tóđǫz bísten órǫ i̧ séđa|
řǫđrígo bá bjén armáđo|

todos espadas ceñidas,   toðos espáðas θeŋíðası

Rodrigo estoque dorado ;   r̄ǫðrígo estóke ðoráðo|

todos con sendas varicas,   tóðǫs kǫn séndaz b̄aríkası

Rodrigo lanza en la ma-   r̄ǫðrígo lánθa en la má-
no ;   no|

todos guantes olorosos,   tóðǫz gwántes olorósǫsı

Rodrigo guante mallado ; r̄ǫðrígo gwánte maḷáðo|

todos sombreros muy ri-   tóðǫs sǫmbrérǫz mwí r̄í-
cos,   kǫsı

Rodrigo casco afilado,   r̄ǫðrígo kásko afilaðoı

y encima del casco lleva yenθíma ðeḷ kásko ḷéb̄aı

un bonete colorado.   úm b̄onéte koloráðo‖

Andando por su camino, andándo pǫr su kamínoı

unos con otros hablando, únǫs kon ótros ab̄lándoı

allegados son a Burgos ; aḷegáðǫs són a b̄úrgǫs|

con el rey se han encon- kon eḷ r̄éi̧ se án eŋkǫn-
trado.   tráðo‖

Los que vienen con el rey lǫs ke b̄jéneŋ kon eḷ r̄éi̧

entre sí van razonando ; entre sí b̄an r̄aθonándo|

unos lo dicen de quedo, únǫz lo ðíθen de kéðo|

otros lo van preguntan- ótrǫz lo b̄ám preguntán-
do :   do|

— Aquí viene entre esta akí   b̄jéne entre ésta
gente   xénte

quien mató al conde Lo- kjen mato ál kǫnde lo-
zano.   θáno‖

Como lo oyera Rodrigo, komo lo oyéra r̄ǫðrígoı

en hito los ha mirado;
con alta y soberbia voz
de esta manera ha ha-
blado:

— Si hay alguno entre
vosotros,
su pariente o adeudado,
que le pese de su muerte,
salga luego a demandallo;
yo se lo defenderé,
quiera a pie, quiera a
caballo.
Todos responden a una:
— Demándelo su pecado.
Todos se apearon juntos
para al rey besar la ma-
no;
Rodrigo solo quedó
encima de su caballo.
Entonces habló su padre,
bien oiréis lo que ha ha-
blado:
— Apeáos vos, mi hijo,
besaréis al rey la mano;
porque él es vuestro se-
ñor

en íto los á miráđo|
kon álta i̯ soƀérƀja ƀǫ́θ
de ésta manéra á a-
ƀláđo|
sj á yalgúno entre
ƀosótrọs|
su parjénte o ađeu̯đáđo
ke le pése đe su mwę́rte|
sálga lwégo a đemandáḷo|
yó se lo đefenderé|
kjéra a pjé| kjéra a
kaƀáḷo||
tóđọz r̄espǫ́nden a úna|
demándelo su pekáđo||
tóđọs se apeárǫŋ xuntọs
para al r̄éi̯ ƀesár la má-
no|
r̄ǫđrígo sólo keđó
enθíma đe su kaƀáḷo||
entǫ́nθes aƀló su páđre|
bjen ọi̯rȩ́i̯s lo ke á a-
ƀláđo|
apeáọz ƀǫ́s| mi íxo|
besarȩ́i̯s al r̄éi̯ la máno|
pǫrke él éz ƀwéstro se-
nǫ́r|

vos, hijo, sois su vasa-
llo.

bǫ̧s₁ ixo₁ sǫ̧is su ƀasá-
lǫ‖

Desque Rodrigo esto oyó,
sintióse más agraviado ;
las palabras que responde
son de hombre muy eno-
jado :
— Si otro me lo dijera,
ya me lo hubiera pagado ;
mas por mandarlo vos,
padre,
yo lo haré de buen grado.

deskę̧ řǫđrígo ésto oyó₁
sintjóse más agraƀjáđo|
las paláƀras kę̧ řespǫ̧́nde
sǫn de ǫ̧mbre mwí enǫ-
xáđo|
si ótro me lo đixéra₁
yá me lo u̧ƀjéra pagáđo|
mas pǫr mandárlo ƀǫ̧́s₁
páđre₁
yo lo aré đe ƀweŋ gráđo‖

Ya se apeaba Rodrigo
para al rey besar la ma-
no ;
al hincar de la rodilla,
el estoque se ha arran-
cado.

yá se apeáƀa řǫđrígo
para al řę̧́i̧ ƀesár la má-
no|
al iŋkár đe la řǫđíḷa
el estóke se á ařaŋ-
káđo‖

Espantóse de esto el rey,
y dijo como turbado :
— Quítate, Rodrigo, allá,
quítateme allá, diablo,
que tienes el gesto
de hombre,
y los hechos de león
bravo.

espantóse đésto ęl řę̧́i̧
i đíxo komo turƀáđo|
kítate řǫđrígo aḷá|
kítateme aḷá điáƀlo|
ke tjénes ęl xésto
đe ǫ̧mbre
i los éçǫz đe leǫ̧́m
bráƀo‖

Como Rodrigo esto oyó,

apriesa pide el caballo;

con una voz alterada,

contra el rey así ha ha-
blado:

— Por besar mano de rey

no me tengo por hon-
rado;

porque la besó mi padre

me tengo por afrentado.

En diciendo estas pala-
bras,

salido se ha del palacio;

consigo se los tornaba

los trescientos hijosdal-
go;

si bien vinieron ves-
tidos,

volvieron mejor arma-
dos;

y si vinieron en mulas,

todos vuelven en caba-
llos.

komọ r̄ọđrígo ésto oyó ǀ

aprjésa píđe ẹl kaƀáḷo ǀ

kon úna ƀóθ alteráđa

kọntra ẹl r̄éi̯ asjá a a-
ƀláđo

pọr ƀesár máno đẹ r̄éi̯

nó me téŋgo por ọn-
r̄áđo ǀ

pọrke la ƀesó mi páđre

me téŋgo por afrentáđo ǁ

en diθjéndo éstas palá-
ƀras

salíđo se á đẹl ·paláθjo ǀ

kọnsígo se lọs tọrnáƀa

lọs tresθjéntos ixọzđál-
go ǁ

si ƀjém binjérọm bes-
tíđọs ǀ

ƀọlƀjérọn mẹxór armá-
đọs ǀ

i si ƀinjéron en múlas

tóđọz ƀwḛḷƀen eŋ kaƀá-
lọs ǁ

CHAPTER IX

PHONETIC TRANSCRIPTIONS OF THE THREE REGULAR CONJUGATIONS AND THE CARDINAL AND ORDINAL NUMBERS

104.

Las tres conjugaciones regulares	las trés kǫŋxugaθjónez r̦eguláres
Primera conjugación	priméra kǫŋxugaθjǫ́n
Infinitivo	im̦finitíƀo
hablar	aƀlár
Indicativo	indikatíƀo
Presente	presénte
hablo	áƀlo
hablas	áƀlas
habla	áƀla
hablamos	aƀlámǫs
habláis	aƀláịs
hablan	áƀlan
Pasado descriptivo o imperfecto	pasáđo đeskríptíƀo ǫ įmpęrfę́kto
hablaba	aƀláƀa
hablabas	aƀláƀas
hablaba	aƀláƀa
hablábamos	aƀláƀamǫs
hablabais	aƀláƀaịs
hablaban	aƀláƀan

114

Las tres conjugaciones regulares	las trés koŋxugaθjónez r̄eguláres
Primera conjugación	priméra koŋxugaθjón
Pasado absoluto o pretérito	pasáđo aƀsolúto o pretérito
hablé	aƀlé
hablaste	aƀláste
habló	aƀló
hablamos	aƀlámǫs
hablasteis	aƀlástẹįs
hablaron	aƀlárǫn
Futuro	futúro
hablaré	aƀlaré
hablarás	aƀlarás
hablará	aƀlará
hablaremos	aƀlarémǫs
hablaréis	aƀlaréįs
hablarán	aƀlarán
Condicional	kǫndiθjonál
hablaría	aƀlaría
hablarías	aƀlarías
hablaría	aƀlaría
hablaríamos	aƀlaríamǫs
hablaríais	aƀlaríaįs
hablarían	aƀlarían

as tres conjugaciones regulares	las trés koŋxugaθjónez r̃eguláres
Primera conjugación	priméra koŋxugaθjǫ́n
Subjuntivo	subxuntíbo
Presente	presénte
hable	áble
hables	ábles
hable	áble
hablemos	ablémǫs
habléis	ablę́i̯s
hablen	áblen
Pasado, primera forma	pasáđo priméra fǫ́rma
hablara	ablára
hablaras	abláras
hablara	ablára
habláramos	abláramǫs
hablarais	ablárai̯s
hablaran	abláran
Pasado, segunda forma	pasádo segúnda fǫ́rma
hablase	abláse
hablases	ablases
hablase	abláse
hablásemos	ablásemǫs
hablaseis	ablásę́i̯s
hablasen	ablásen
Imperativo	imperatíbo
habla	ábla
hablad	abláđ

Las tres conjugaciones regulares	las trés koŋxugaθjónez r̦eguláres
Segunda conjugación	segúnda koŋxugaθjǫ̃n
Infinitivo	im̩finitíbo
ceder	θeđę́r
Indicativo	indikatíbo
Presente	presénte
cedo	θéđo
cedes	θéđes
cede	θéđe
cedemos	θeđémǫs
cedéis	θeđę́įs
ceden	θéđen
Pasado descriptivo o imperfecto	pasáđo đeskriptíbo ǫ̃ im̩pęrfę́kto
cedía	θeđía
cedías	θeđías
cedía	θeđía
cedíamos	θeđíamǫs
cedíais	θeđíaįs
cedían	θeđían

NOTE. — The student should bear in mind that throughout these conjugations the phonetic transcriptions indicate the pronunciation of isolated forms. In connected discourse all initial and final consonants and vowels are subject, of course, to the various changes involved in phonetic syllabication, §§ 10, 76–78, synalepha, §§ 79–83, syneresis, § 84, and other phenomena already discussed.

Las tres conjugaciones regulares	las trés koŋxugaθjónez řẹguláres
Segunda conjugación	segúnda koŋxugaθjǫ́n
Pasado absoluto o pretérito	pasáđo absolúto o pretérito
cedí	θeđí
cediste	θeđíste
cedió	θeđjó
cedimos	θeđímǫs
cedisteis	θeđíste̞is
cedieron	θeđjérǫn
Futuro	futúro
cederé	θeđeré
cederás	θeđerás
cederá	θeđerá
cederemos	θeđerémǫs
cederéis	θeđeréi̞s
cederán	θeđerán
Condicional	kǫndiθjonál
cedería	θeđería
cederías	θeđerías
cedería	θeđería
cederíamos	θeđeríamǫs
cederíais	θeđeríai̞s
cederían	θeđerían

Las tres conjugaciones regulares	las trés koŋxugaθjónez r̦eguláres
Segunda conjugación	segúnda koŋxugaθjǫ́n
Subjuntivo	subxuntíbo
Presente	presénte
ceda	θéđa
cedas	θéđas
ceda	θéđa
cedamos	θeđámǫs
cedáis	θeđáịs
cedan	θéđan
Pasado, primera forma	pasáđo priméra fǫ́rma
cediera	θeđjéra
cedieras	θeđjéras
cediera	θeđjéra
cediéramos	θeđjéramǫs
cedierais	θejérạịs
cedieran	θeđjéran
Pasado, segunda forma	pasáđo segúnda fǫ́rma
cediese	θeđjése
cedieses	θeđjéses
cediese	θeđjése
cediésemos	θeđjésemǫs
cedieseis	θeđjésẹịs
cediesen	θeđjésen
Imperativo	imperatíbo
cede	θéđe
ceded	θeđéđ

Las tres conjugaciones regulares	las trés koŋxugaθjónez r̥eguláres
Tercera conjugación	terθéra koŋxugaθjón
Infinitivo	iɱfinitíbo
vivir	[1] bibír
Indicativo	indikatíbo
Presente	presénte
vivo	[1] bíbo
vives	bíbes
vive	bíbe
vivimos	bibímos
vivís	bibís
viven	bíben
Pasado descriptivo o imperfecto	pasáđo đeskríptíbo o̜ imperfékto
vivía	[1] bibía
vivías	bibías
vivía	bibía
vivíamos	bibíamo̜s
vivíais	bibíai̜s
vivían	bibían

[1] These initial consonants are pronounced as explosives between pauses (initial in the phonic group). If the words are pronounced in rapid succession and with no pauses, all these consonants, with the exception of the initial consonant of the first form in each tense,

Las tres conjugaciones regulares	las trés koŋxugaθjónez r̨eguláres
Tercera conjugación	terθéra koŋxugaθjǫ́n
Pasado absoluto o pretérito	pasáđo aƀsolúto o pretérito
viví	[1] biƀí
viviste	biƀiste
vivió	biƀjó
vivimos	biƀímǫs
vivisteis	biƀístęįs
vivieron	biƀjérǫn
Futuro	futúro
viviré	[1] biƀiré
vivirás	biƀirás
vivirá	biƀirá
viviremos	biƀirémǫs
viviréis	biƀiréįs
vivirán	biƀirán
Condicional	kǫndiθjonál
viviría	[1] biƀiría
vivirías	biƀirías
viviría	biƀiría
viviríamos	biƀiríamǫs
viviríais	biƀiríaįs
vivirían	biƀirían

may be pronounced as continuants: bíƀo ƀíƀez ƀíƀe, etc., biƀiré ƀiƀiráz ƀiƀirá, etc. See also page 122.

Las tres conjugaciones regulares	las trés kǫŋxugaθjónez r̨eguláres
Tercera conjugación	tęrθéra kǫŋxugaθjǫ́n
Subjuntivo	suƀxuntíƀo
Presente	presénte
viva	[1] bíƀa
vivas	bíƀas
viva	bíƀa
vivamos	biƀámǫs
viváis	biƀái̯s
vivan	bíƀan
Pasado, primera forma	pasáđo priméra fǫ́rma
viviera	[1] biƀjéra
vivieras	biƀjéras
viviera	biƀjéra
viviéramos	biƀjéramǫs
vivierais	biƀjérai̯s
vivieran	ƀiƀjéran
Pasado, segunda forma	pasáđo segúnda fǫ́rma
viviese	[1] biƀjése
vivieses	biƀjéses
viviese	biƀjése
viviésemos	biƀjésemǫs
vivieseis	biƀjésęi̯s
viviesen	biƀjésen
Imperativo	imperatíƀo
vive	[1] bíƀe
vivid	biƀíđ

105.

Los números cardinales	loz númeroṣ karđináles
1 uno	úno
2 dos	[1] dǫs
3 tres	trés
4 cuatro	kwátro
5 cinco	θíŋko
6 seis	sé̦is
7 siete	sjéte
8 ocho	óĉo
9 nueve	nwéƀe
10 diez	[1] dję́θ
11 once	ǫ́nθe
12 doce	[1] dóθe
13 trece	tréθe
14 catorce	katǫ́rθe
15 quince	kínθe
16 dieciséis	[1] djeθisé̦is
17 diecisiete	[1] djeθɪsjéte
18 dieciocho	[1] djeθjóĉo
19 diecinueve	[1] djeθinwéƀe
20 veinte	[1] bé̦inte
21 veintiuno	[1] be̦intjúno
22 veintidós	[1] be̦intiđǫ́s
23 veintitrés	[1] be̦intitrés

[1] These initial consonants are thus pronounced (explosives) between pauses (initial in the phonic group). If the numbers are read so that they are not initial in the phonic group they are pronounced as continuants.

Los números cardinales	lọz númerọs karđináles
24 veinticuatro	[1] bẹintikwátro
25 veinticinco	[1] bẹintiθíŋko
26 veintiséis	[1] bẹintiséịs
27 veintisiete	[1] bẹintisjéte
28 veintiocho	[1] bẹintjóĉo
29 veintinueve	[1] bẹintinwéƀe
30 treinta	trẹínta
31 treinta y uno	trẹinta yúno
32 treinta y dos	trẹintaị đós
33 treinta y tres	trẹintaị trés
34 treinta y cuatro	trẹintaị kwátro
35 treinta y cinco	trẹintaị θíŋko
36 treinta y seis	trẹintaị séịs
37 treinta y siete	trẹintaị sjéte
38 treinta y ocho	trẹinta yóĉo
39 treinta y nueve	trẹintaị nwéƀe
40 cuarenta	kwarenta
41 cuarenta y uno	kwarénta yúno
50 cincuenta	θiŋkwénta
60 sesenta	sesénta
70 setenta	seténta
80 ochenta	oĉénta
90 noventa	noƀénta
100 ciento	θjénto
101 ciento uno	θjénto úno

[1] These initial consonants are thus pronounced (explosives) between pauses (initial in the phonic group). If the numbers are read so that they are not initial in the phonic group they are pronounced as continuants.

1000 mil	míl
2000 dos mil	[1] dǫz mil
mil quinientos ochenta y tres	míl kinjéntos oĉéntai̯ trés
un millón seiscientos mil	un milǫ́n sé̦i̦sǝjéntǫs míl

106.

Los números ordinales	lǫz números ǫrđináles
primero	priméro
segundo	segúndo
tercero	te̦rθéro
cuarto	kwárto
quinto	kínto
sexto	sésto
séptimo	sétimo
octavo	ǫktáƀo
noveno	noƀéno
décimo	[1] déθimo
undécimo	undéθimo
duodécimo	[1] dwođéθimo
décimo tercero	[1] deθimo te̦rθéro
décimo cuarto	[1] deθimo kwárto
décimo quinto	[1] deθimo kínto
vigésimo	[1] ƀixésimo
centésimo	θentésimo
milésimo	milésimo

[1] These initial consonants are thus pronounced (explosives) between pauses (initial in the phonic group). If the numbers are read so that they are not initial in the phonic group they are pronounced as continuants.

ANALYTICAL INDEX

The numbers refer to the sections

The numbers refer to the sections

The numbers refer to the sections